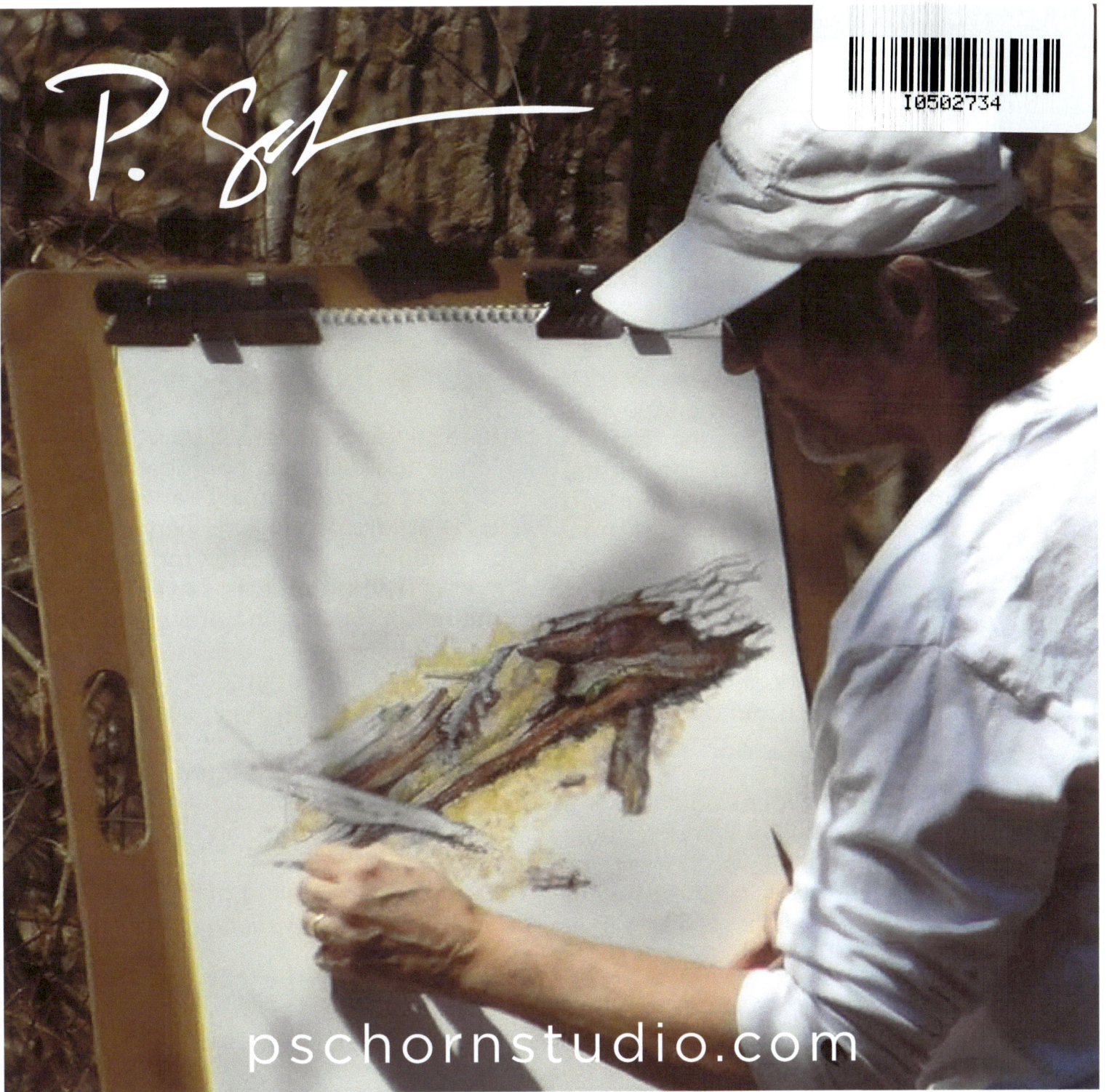

pschornstudio.com

I am a color pencil artist that paints with the pencil

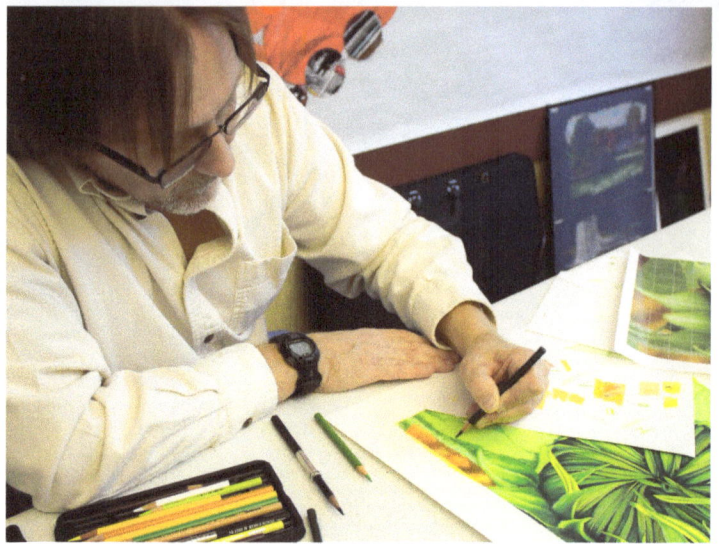

My botanical renderings are not drawings of plant specimens as seen in scientific books, rather, they are renderings of plants as seen through the eye of an artist. I can look at the ground and can see the shapes, light and shadows. I typically do not draw the entire location.

I focus on a portion of the scene and what makes that interesting. Whether that be the individual leaf, flower, or snapshot of the ground, I bring the details to life.

In my drawings, I focus on achieving realism and try to put in as much detail as possible. I want the viewer to look and then get lost in the scene as if they were standing in it.

After attending Eastern Illinois University on an Art Scholarship, I graduated with a BA, double majoring in Graphic Design and 2D Studio Art. I have been an independent graphic artist for more than 30 years. Throughout those years, I continued to paint and draw.

With much encouragement from my family, I started drawing in earnest several years ago and have not stopped. I have been featured in two art publications and have done many solo & group exhibits, demos, and workshops.

This book is a sampling of my art - *hope you enjoy it as much as I do.*

pschornstudio.com

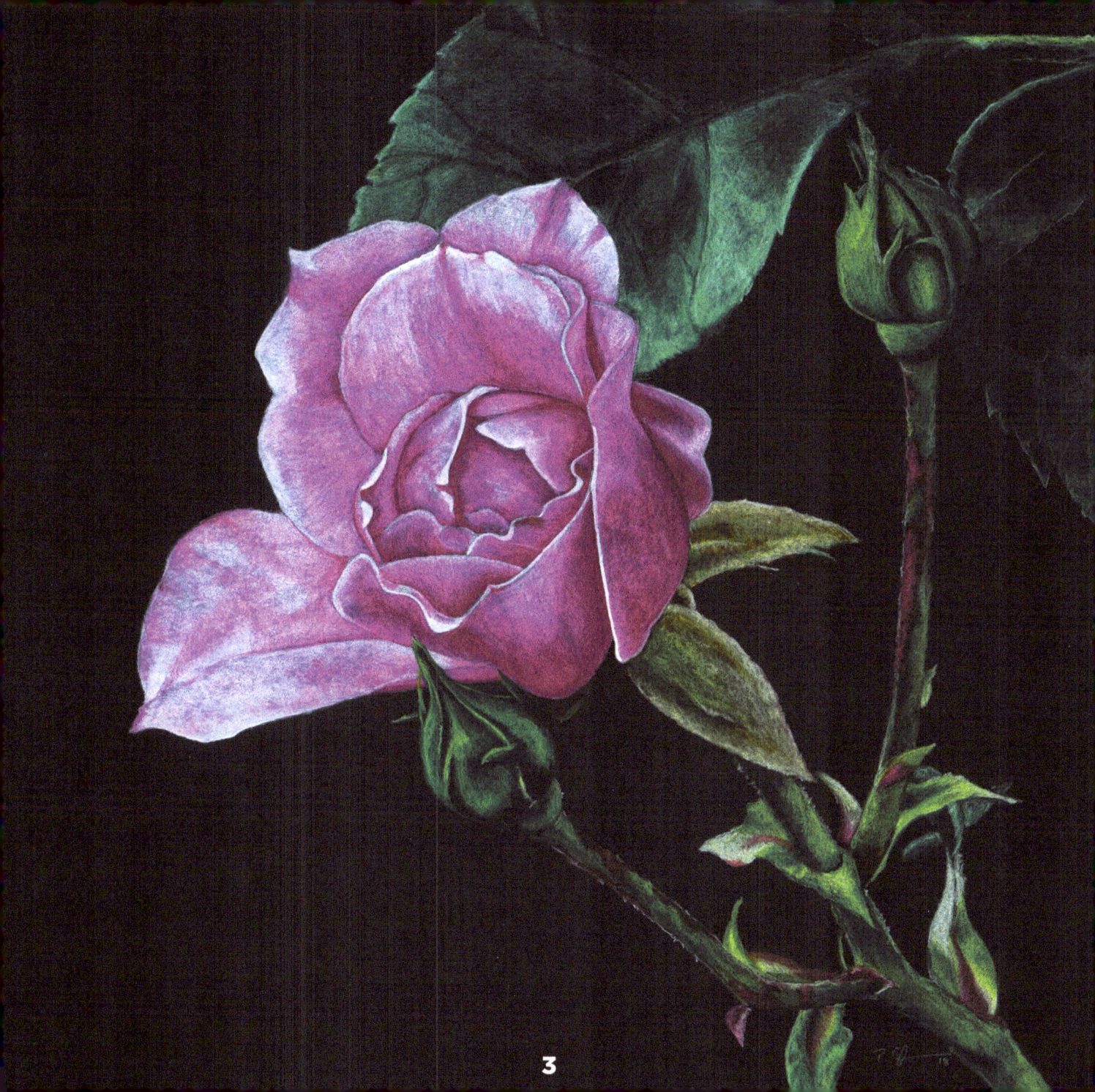

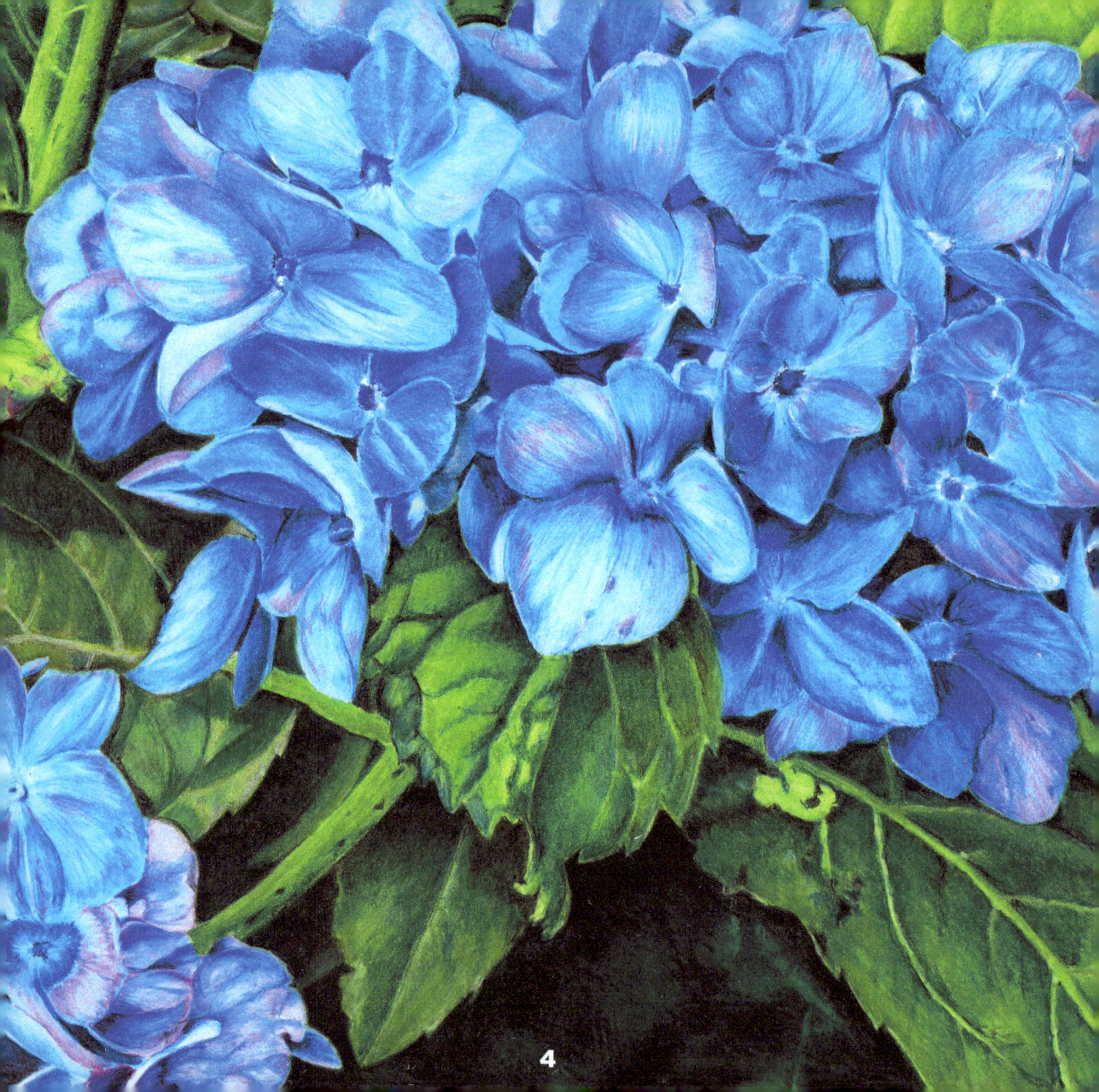

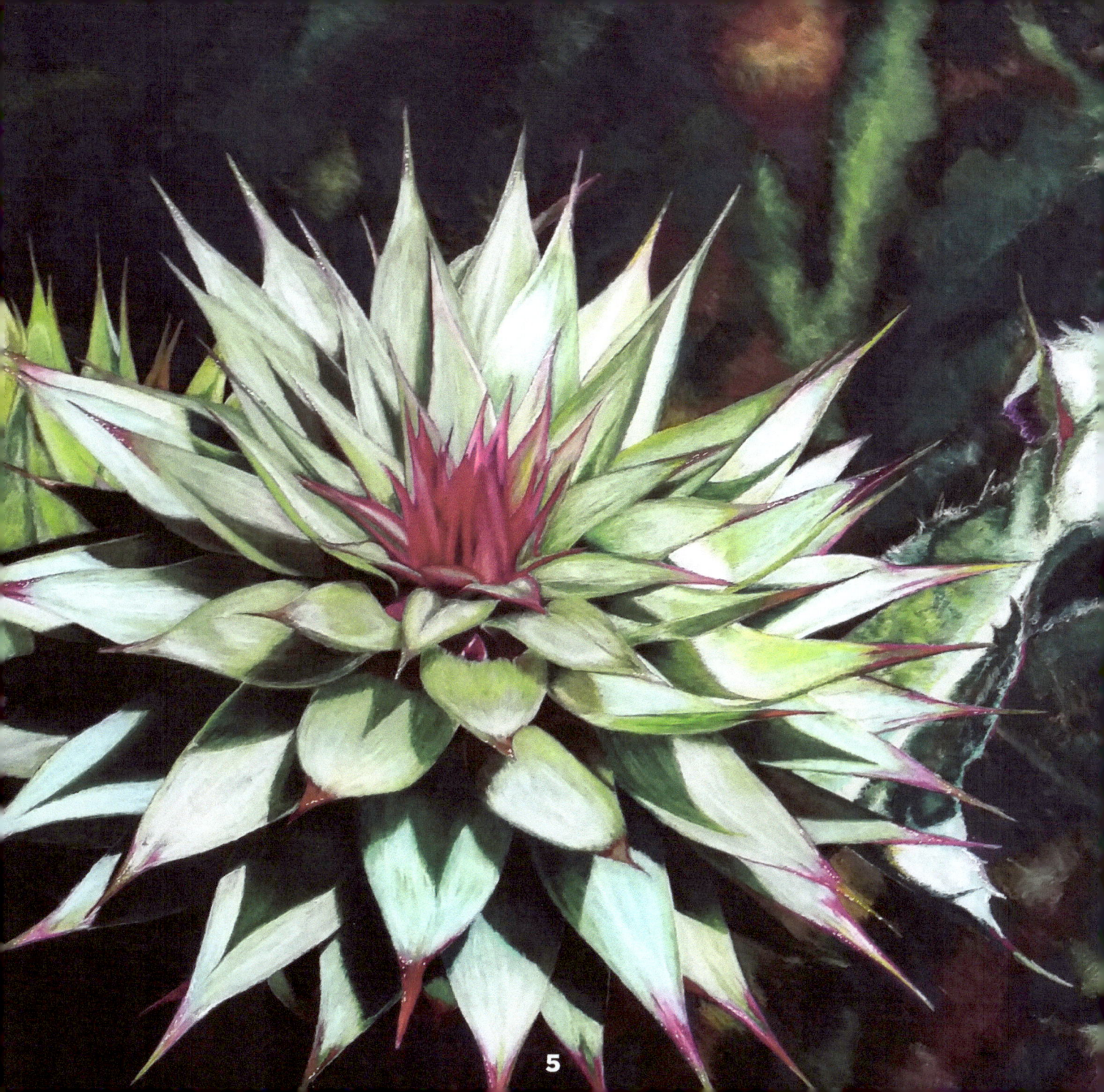

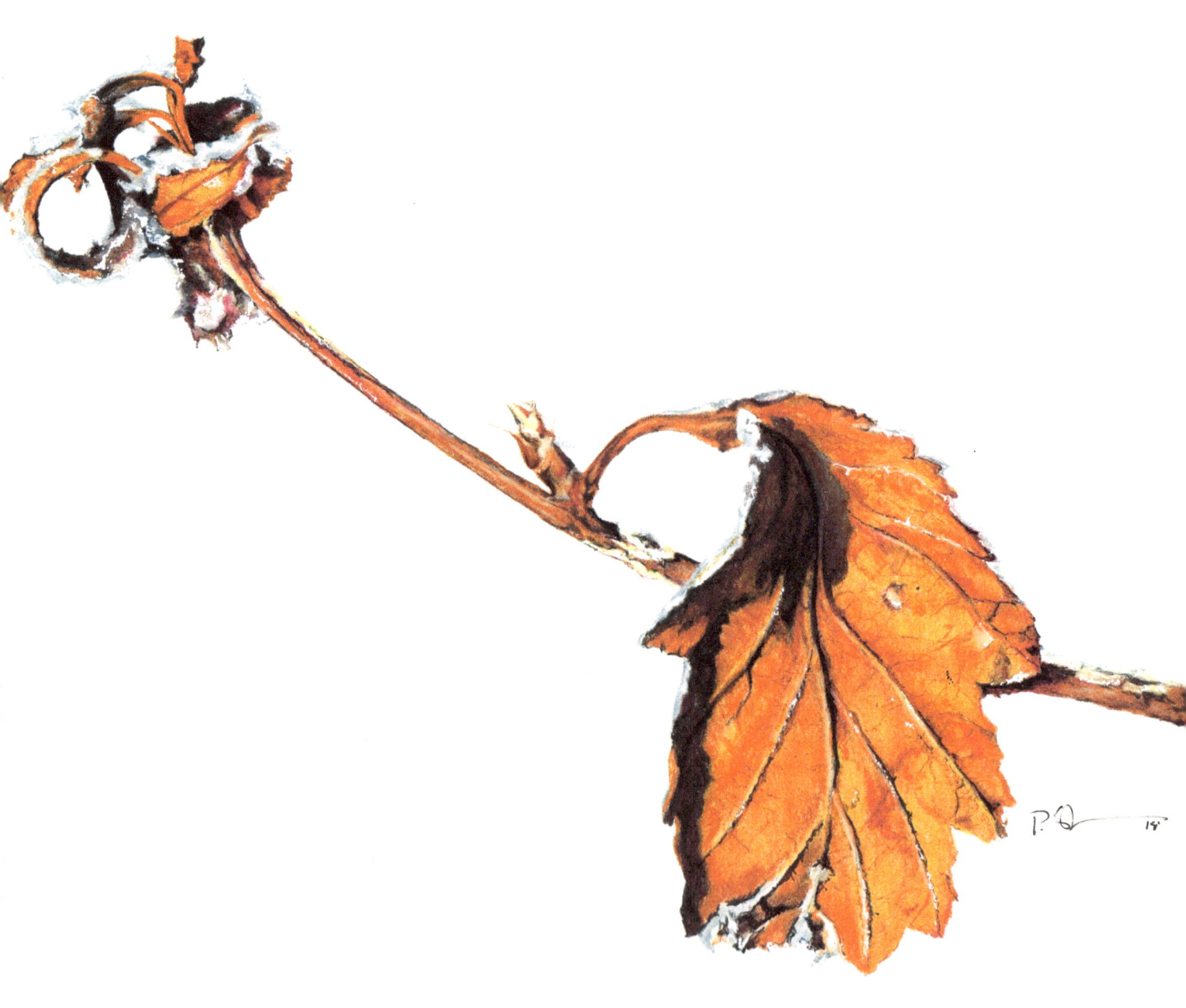

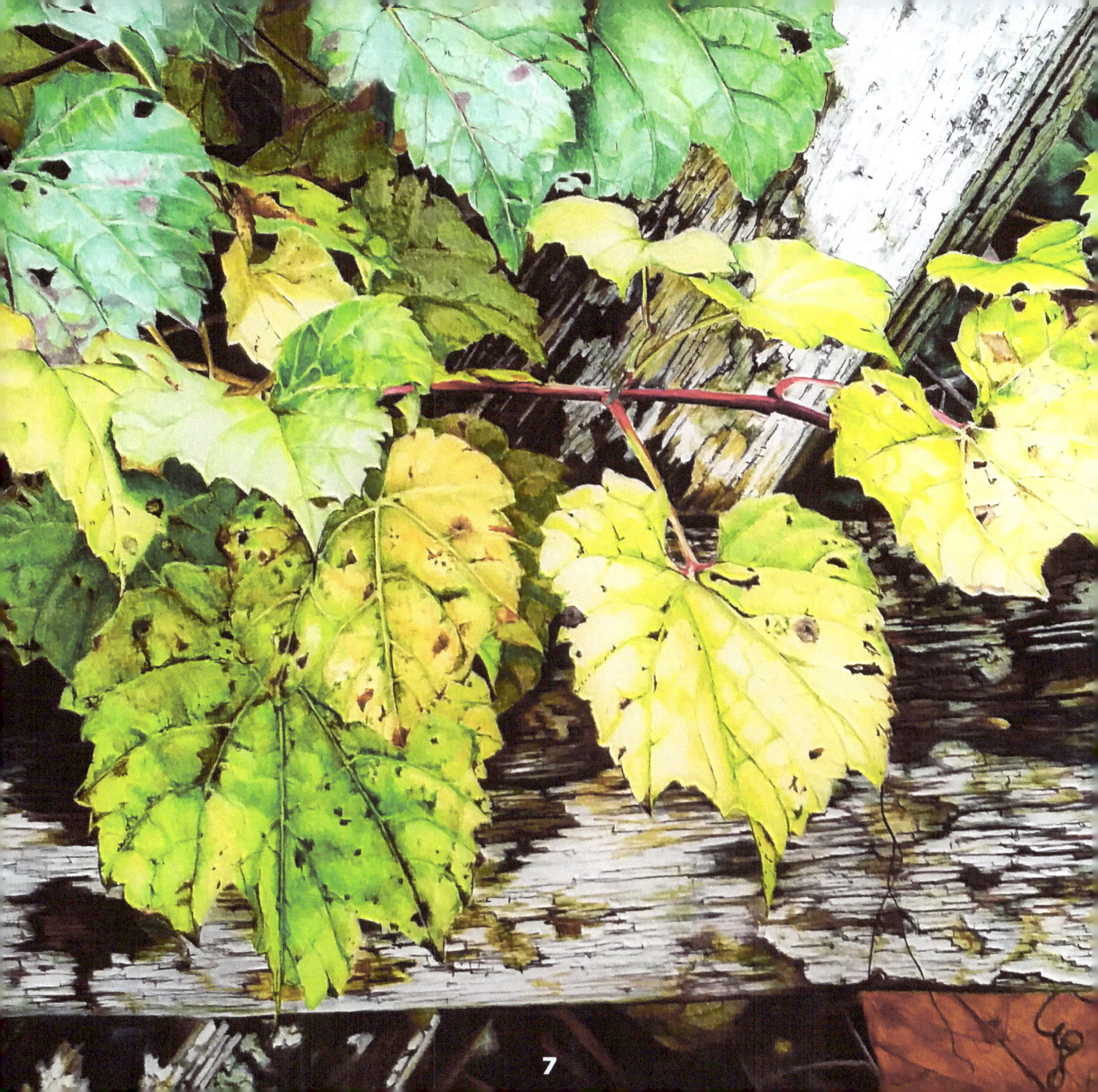

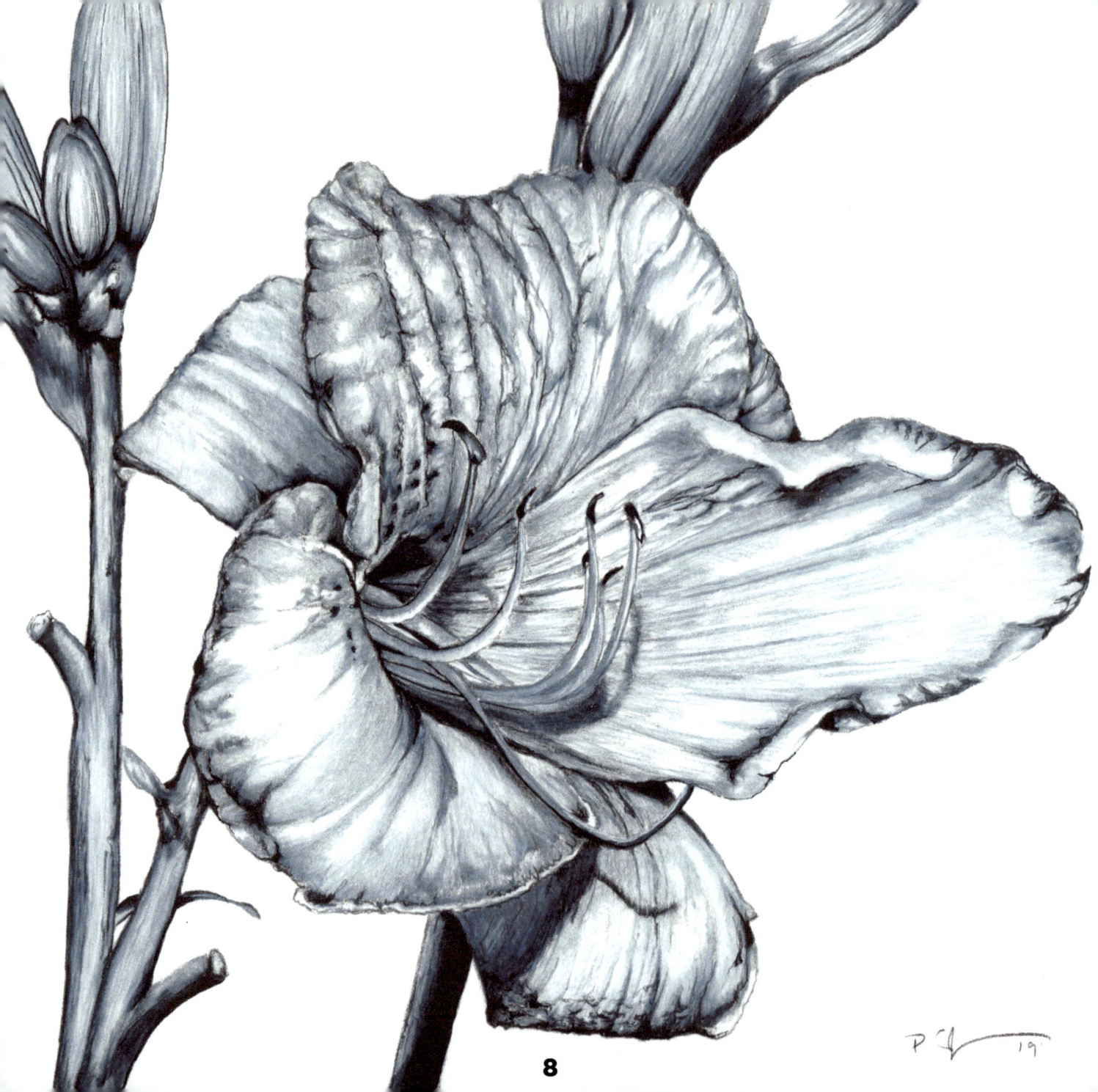

8

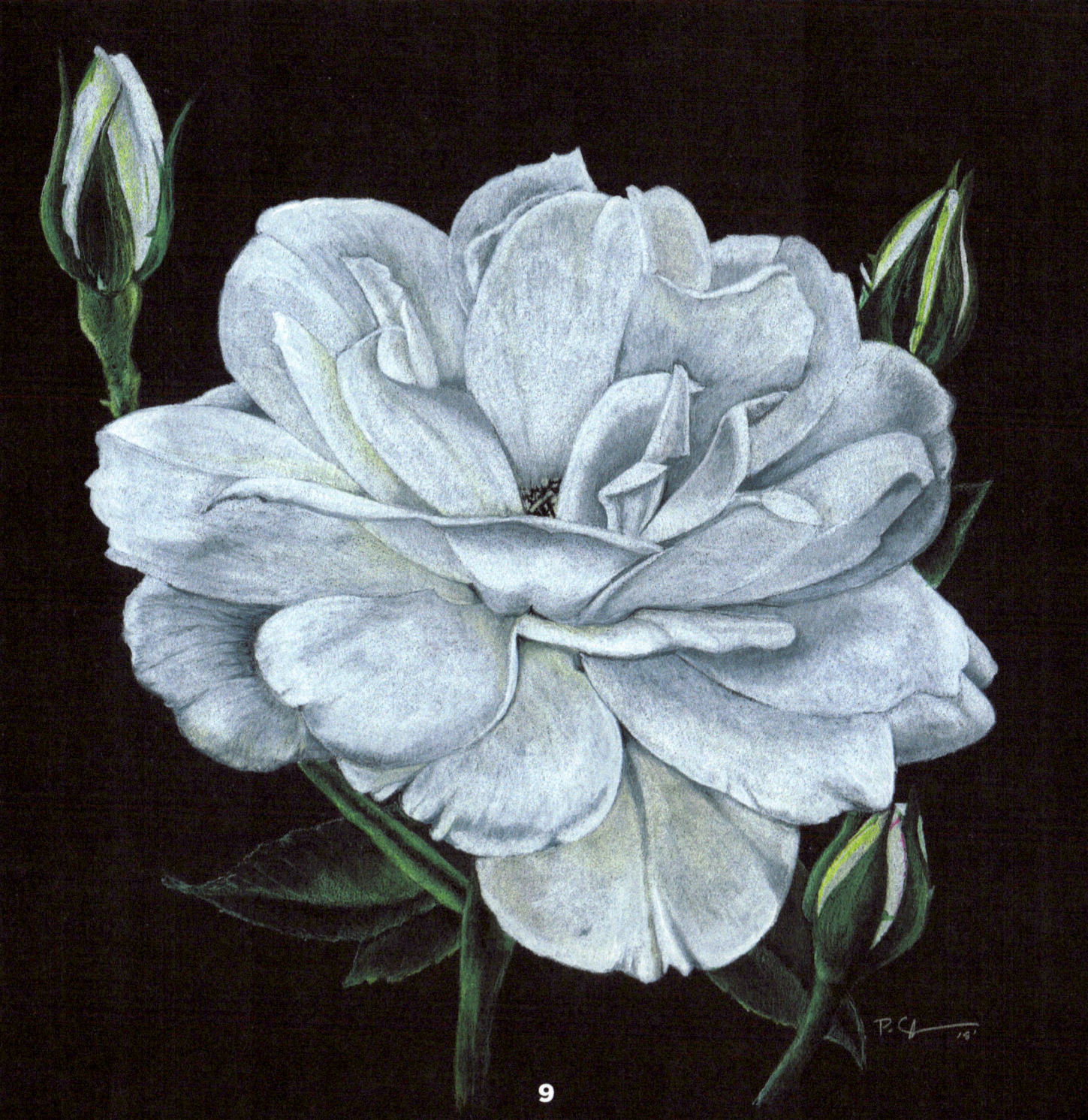

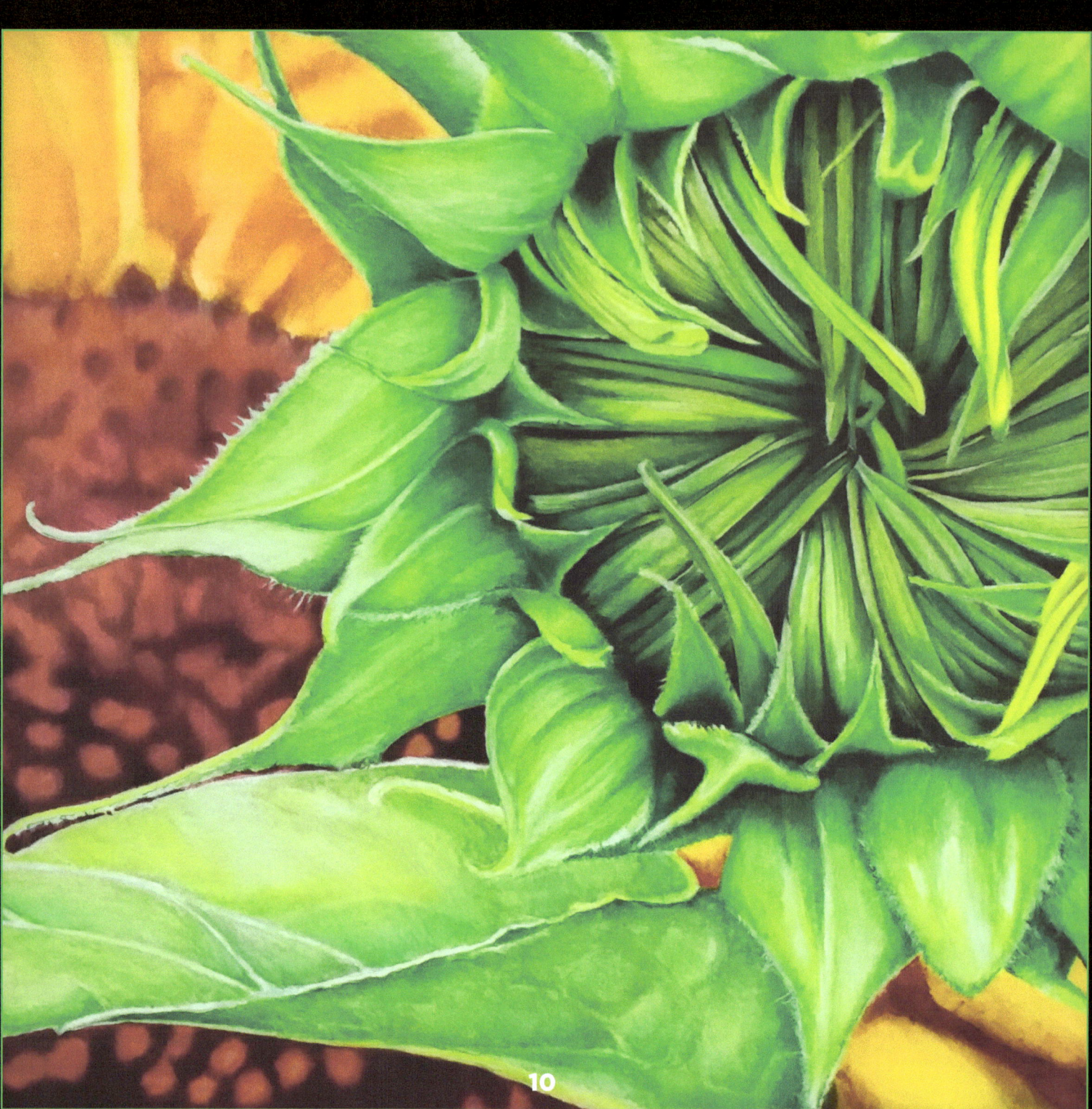

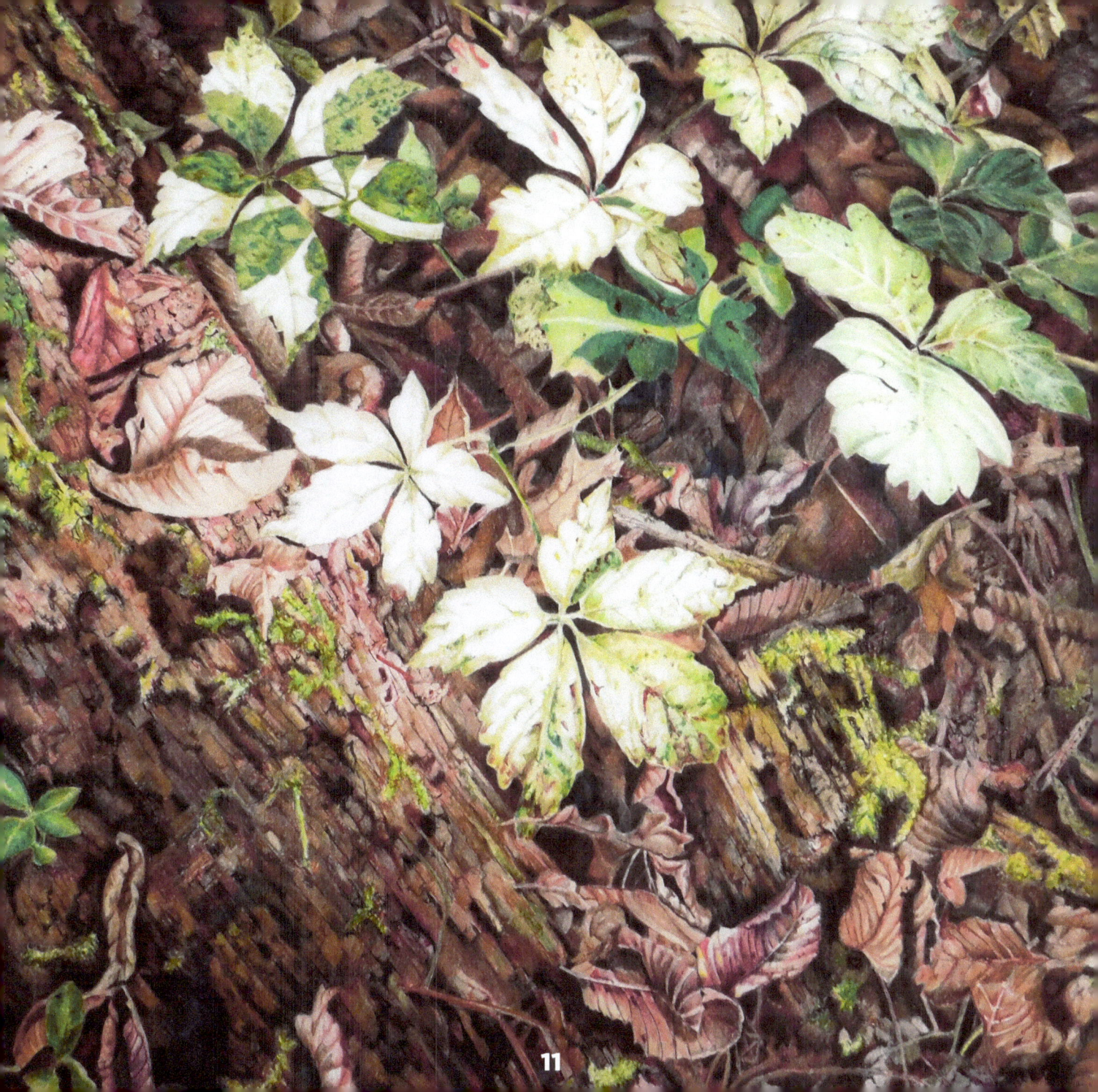

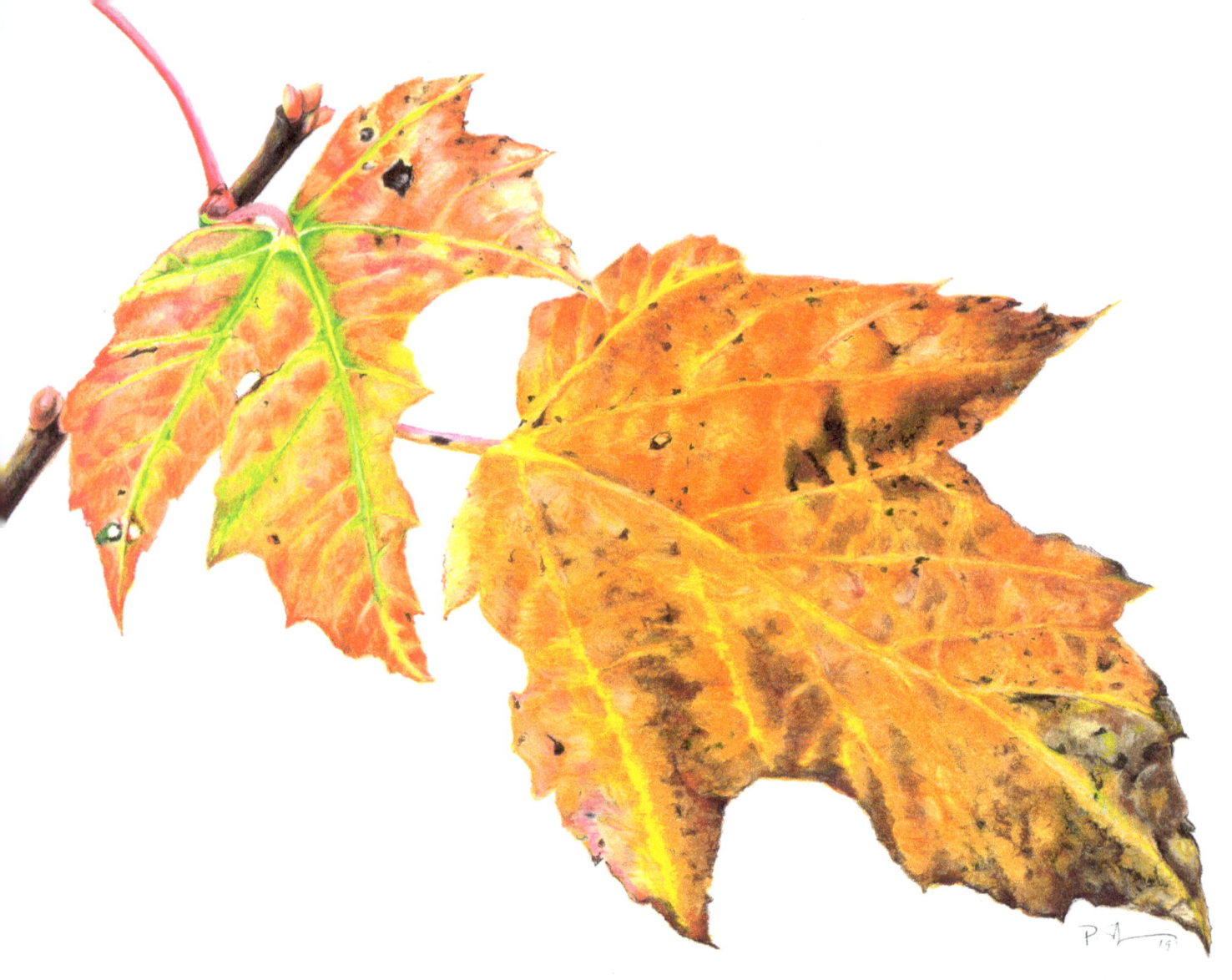

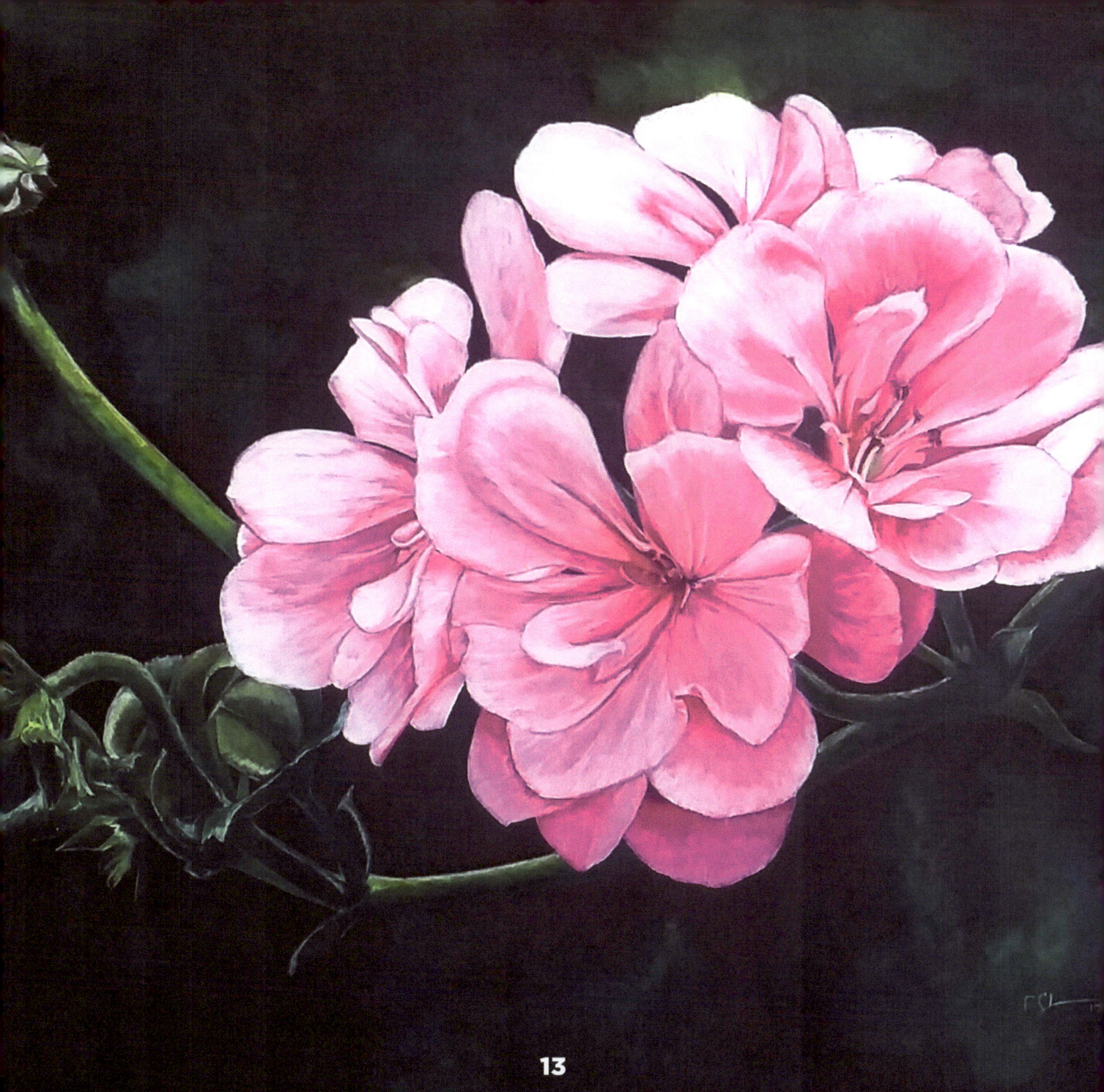

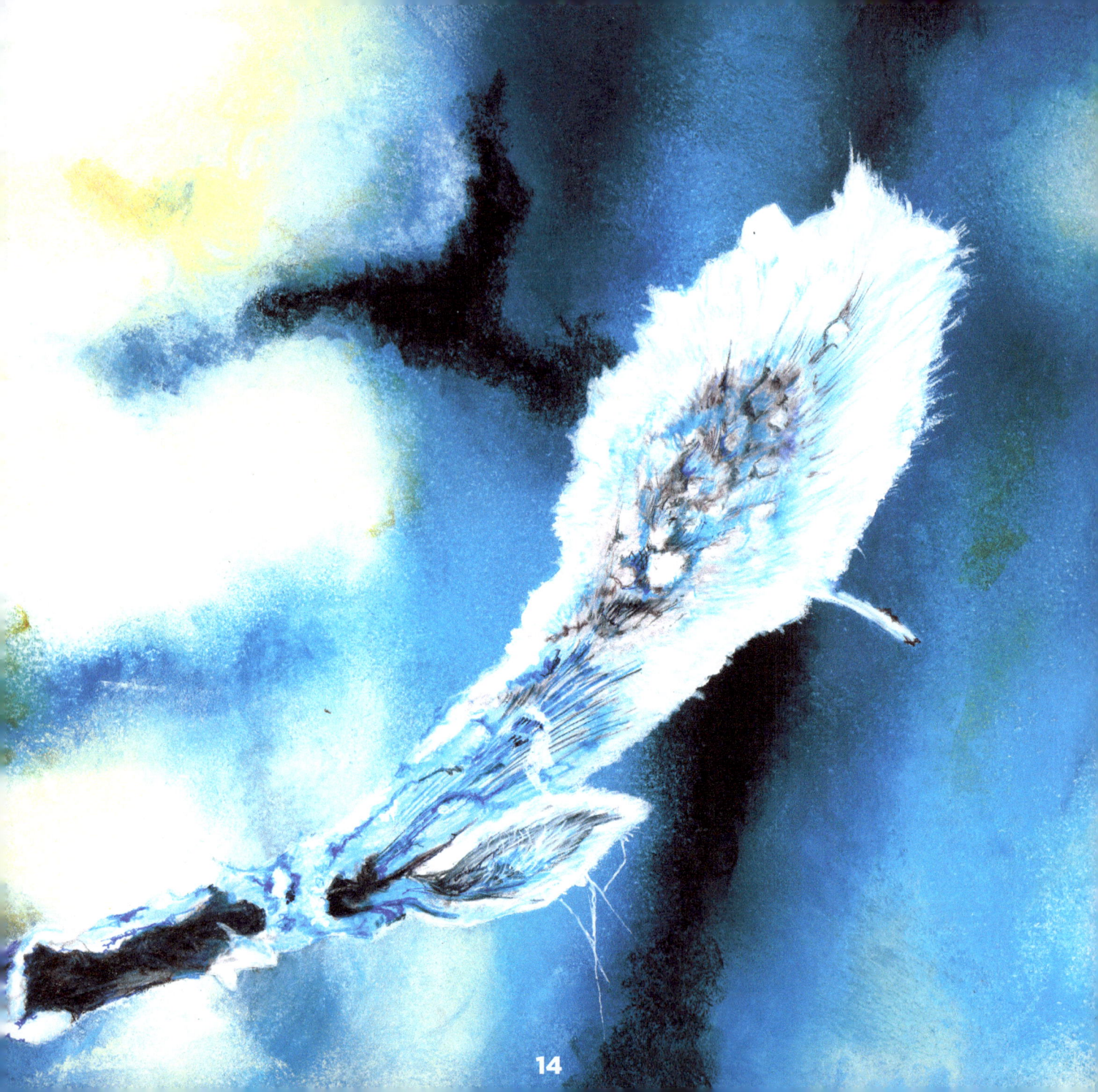

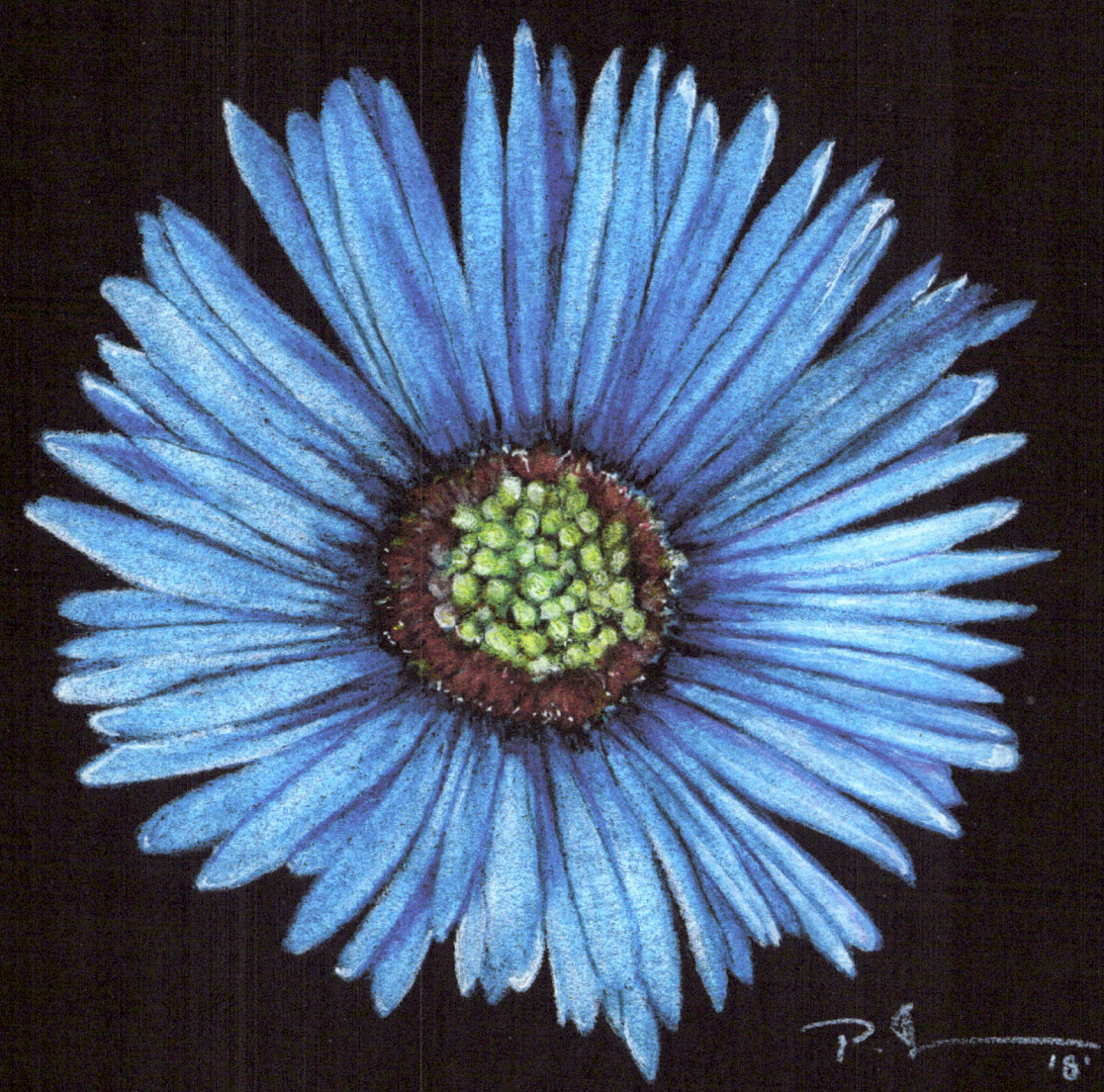

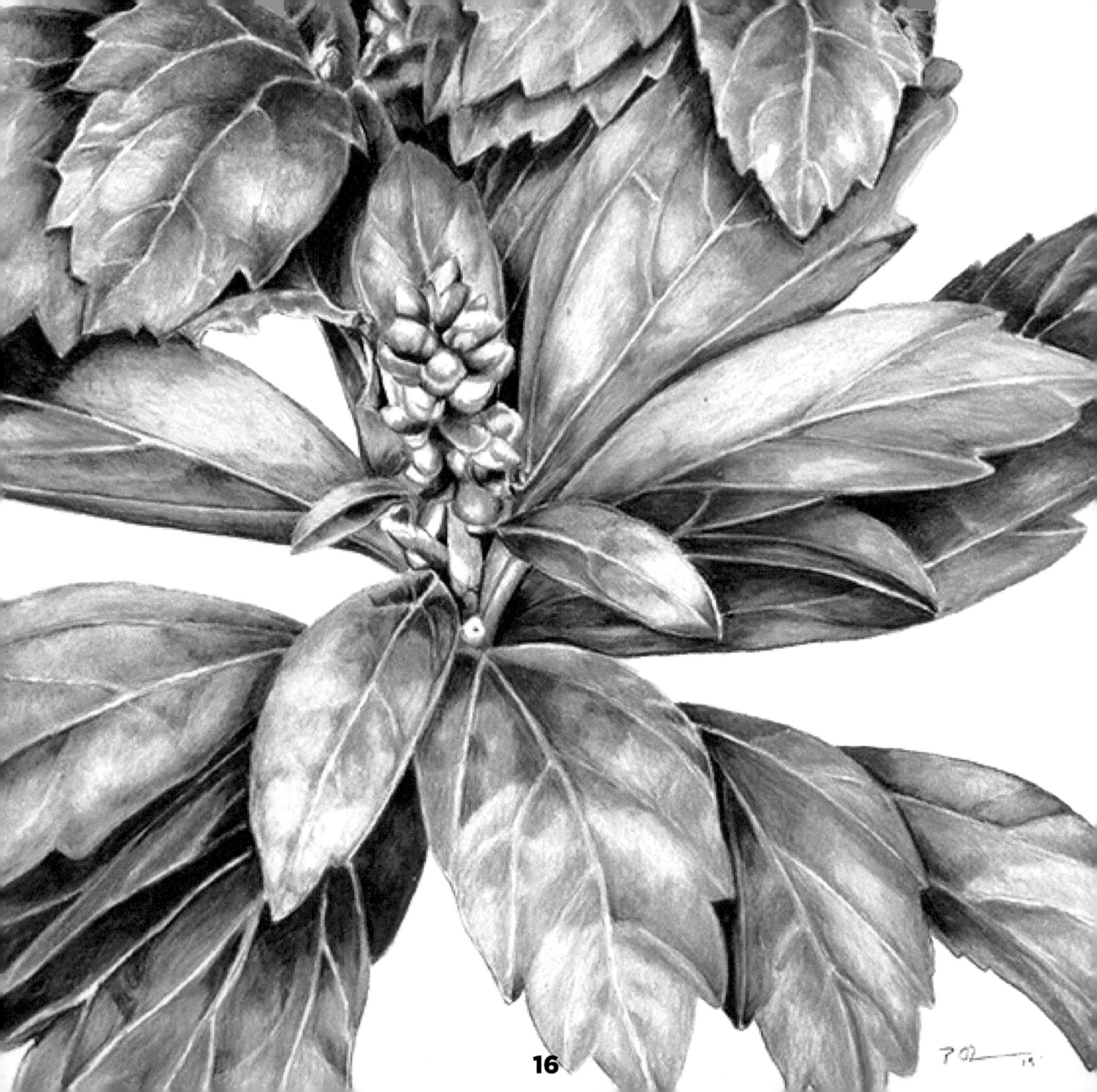

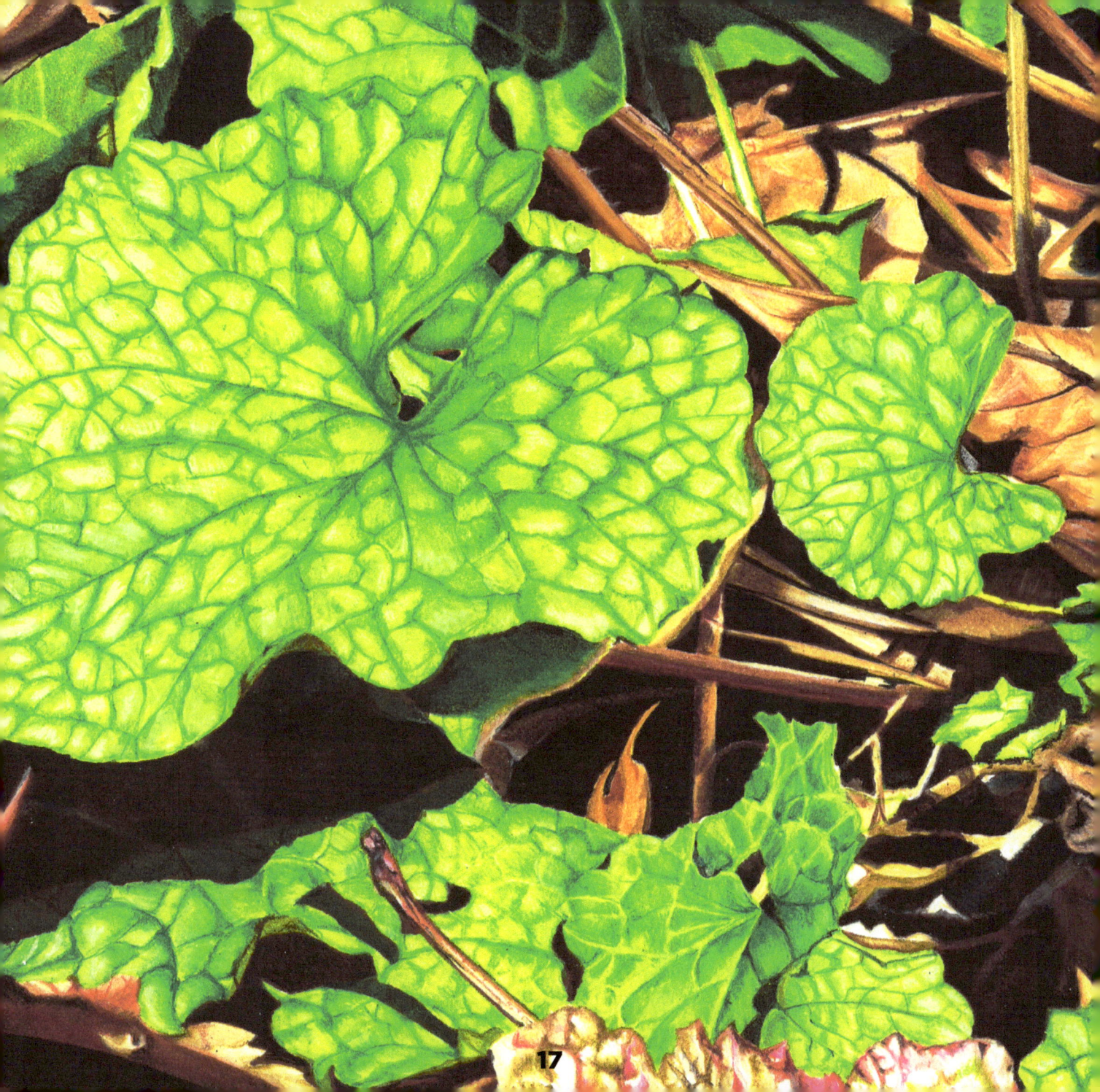

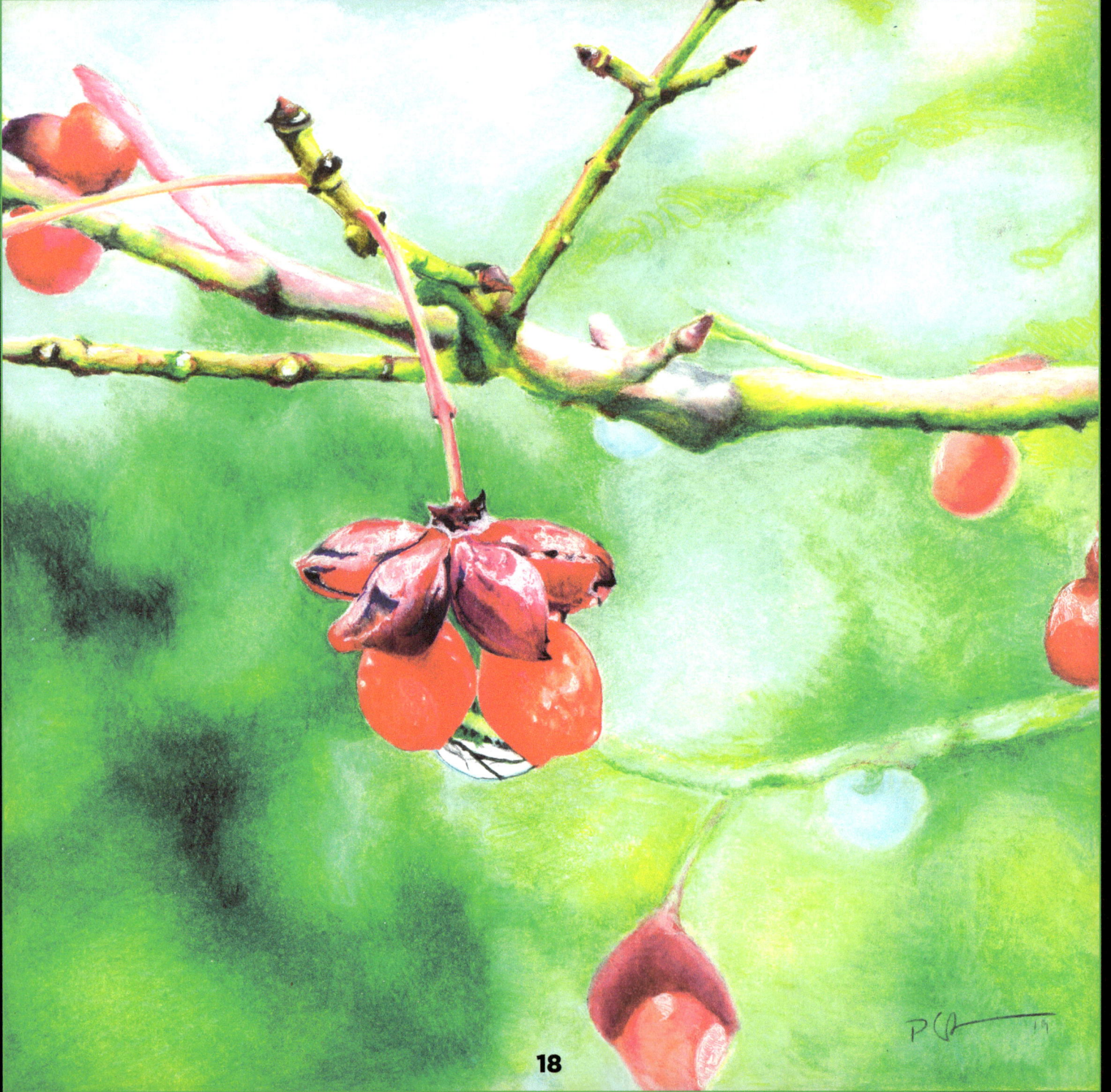

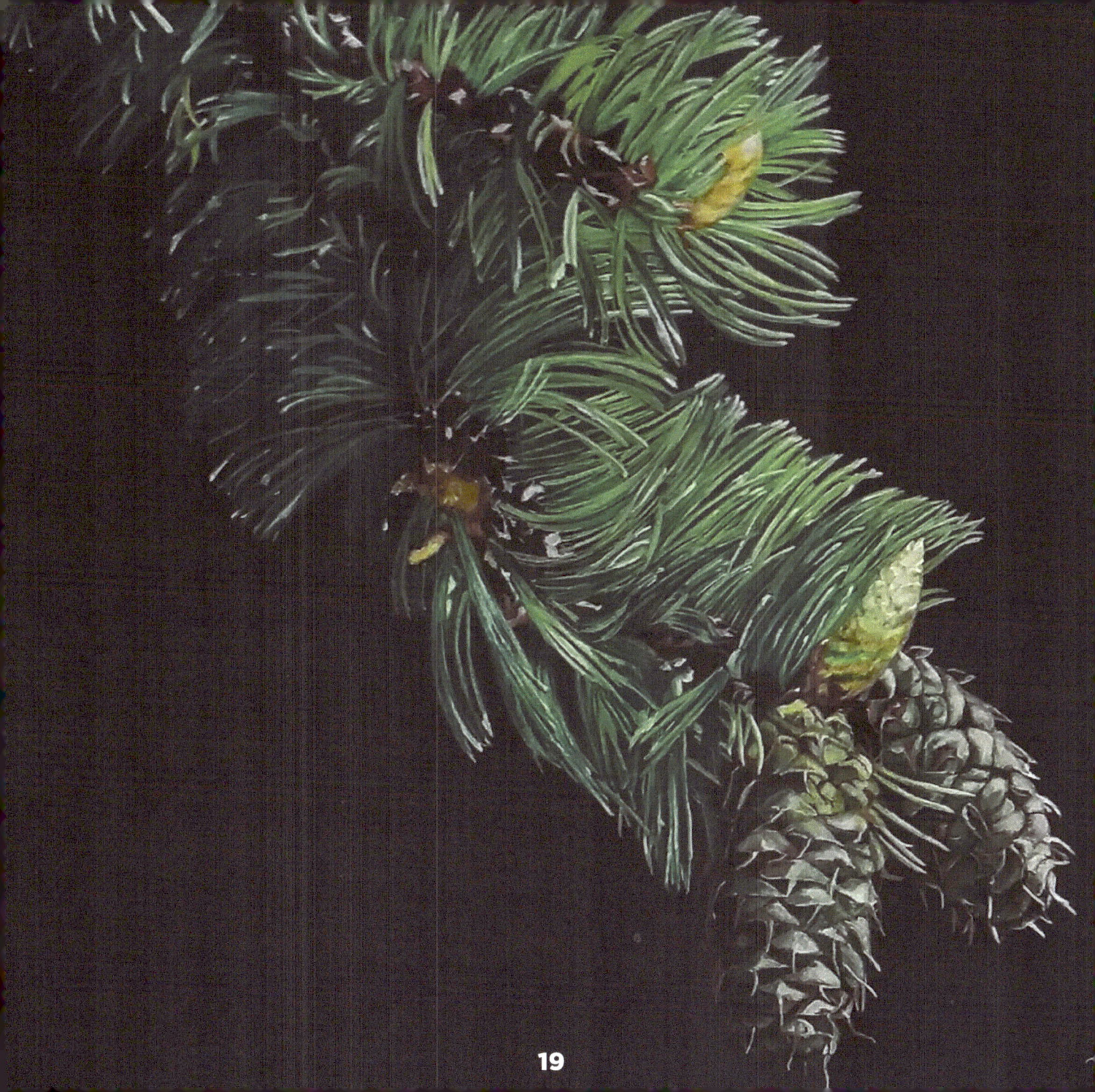

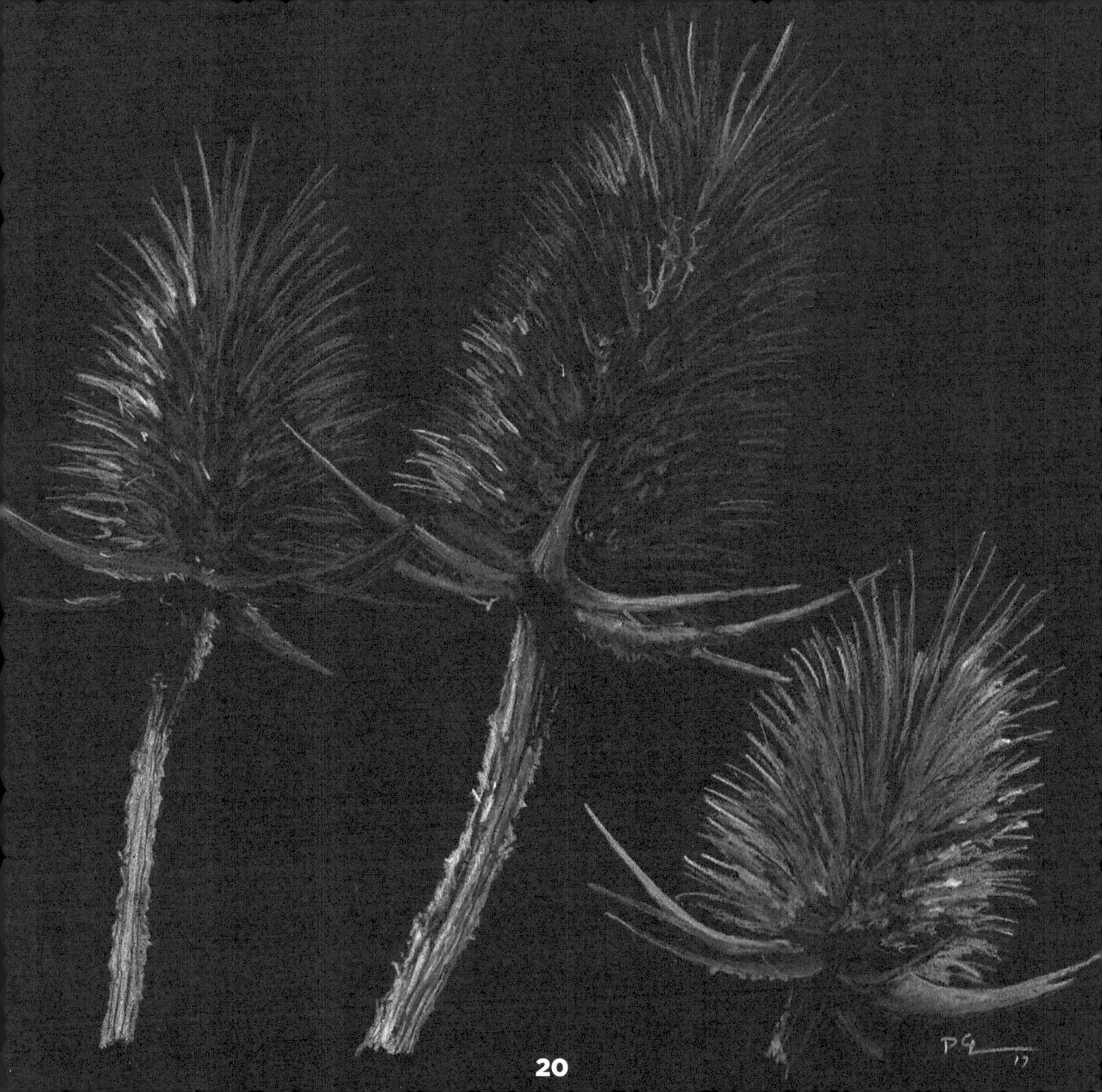

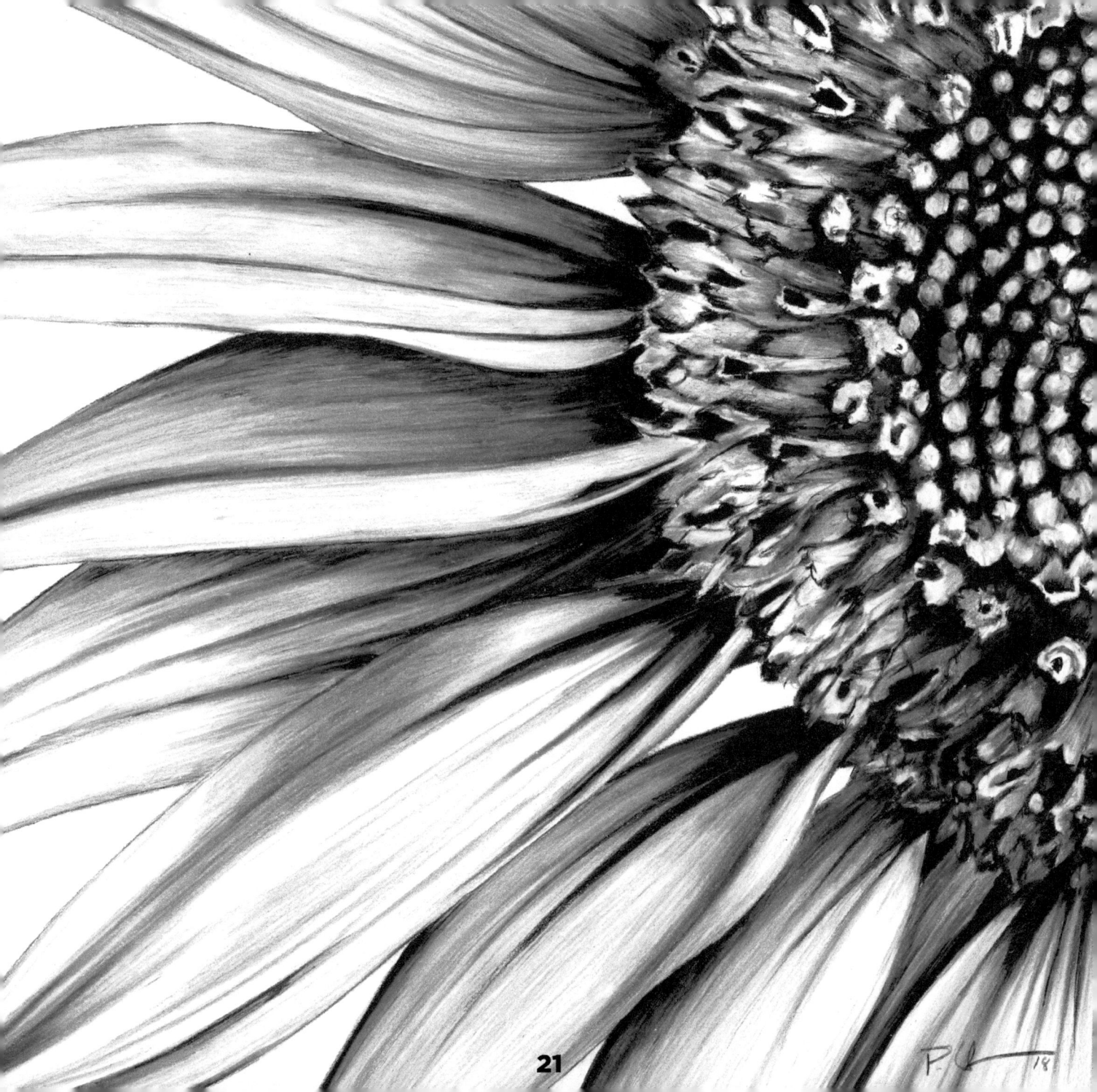

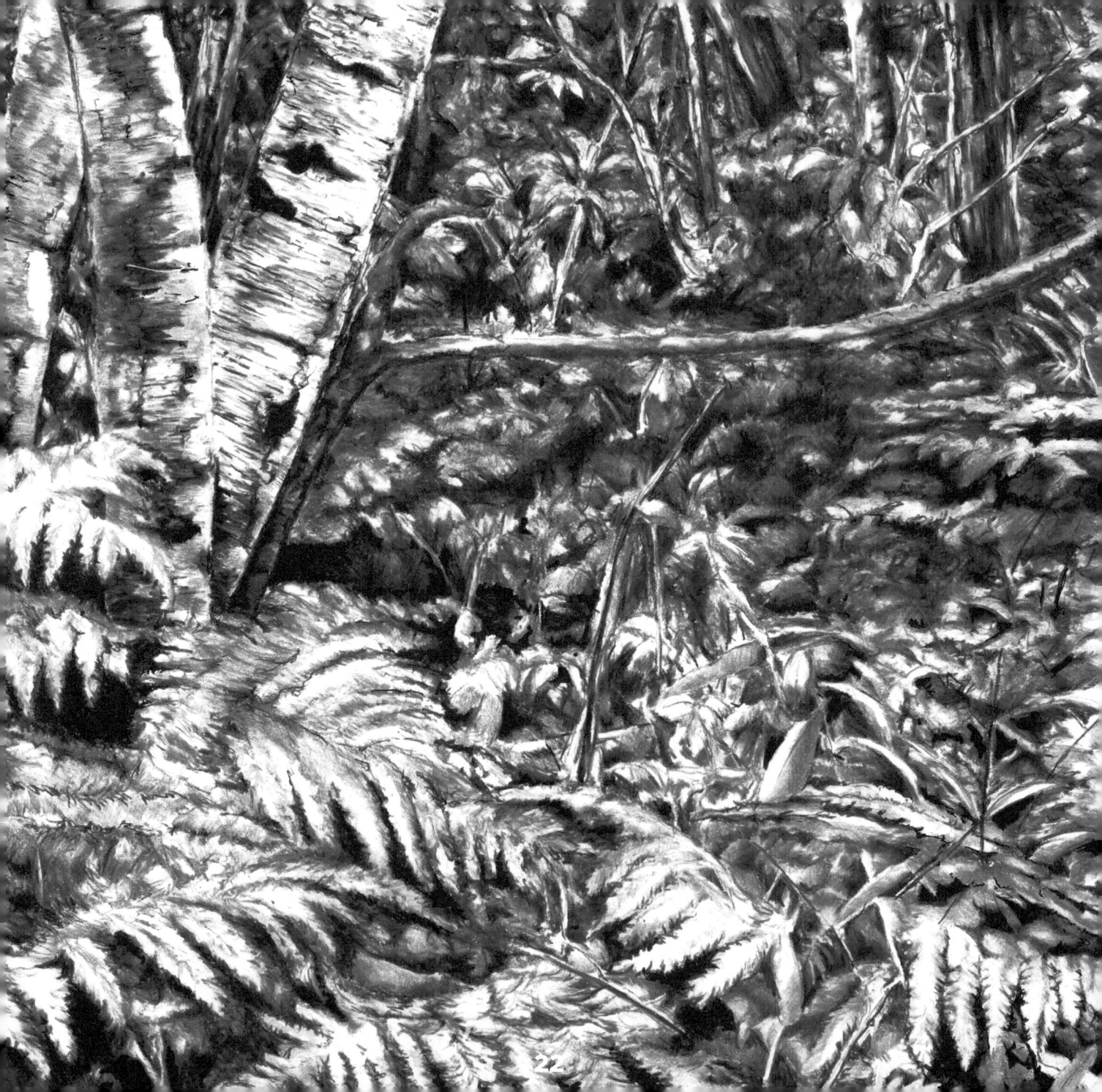

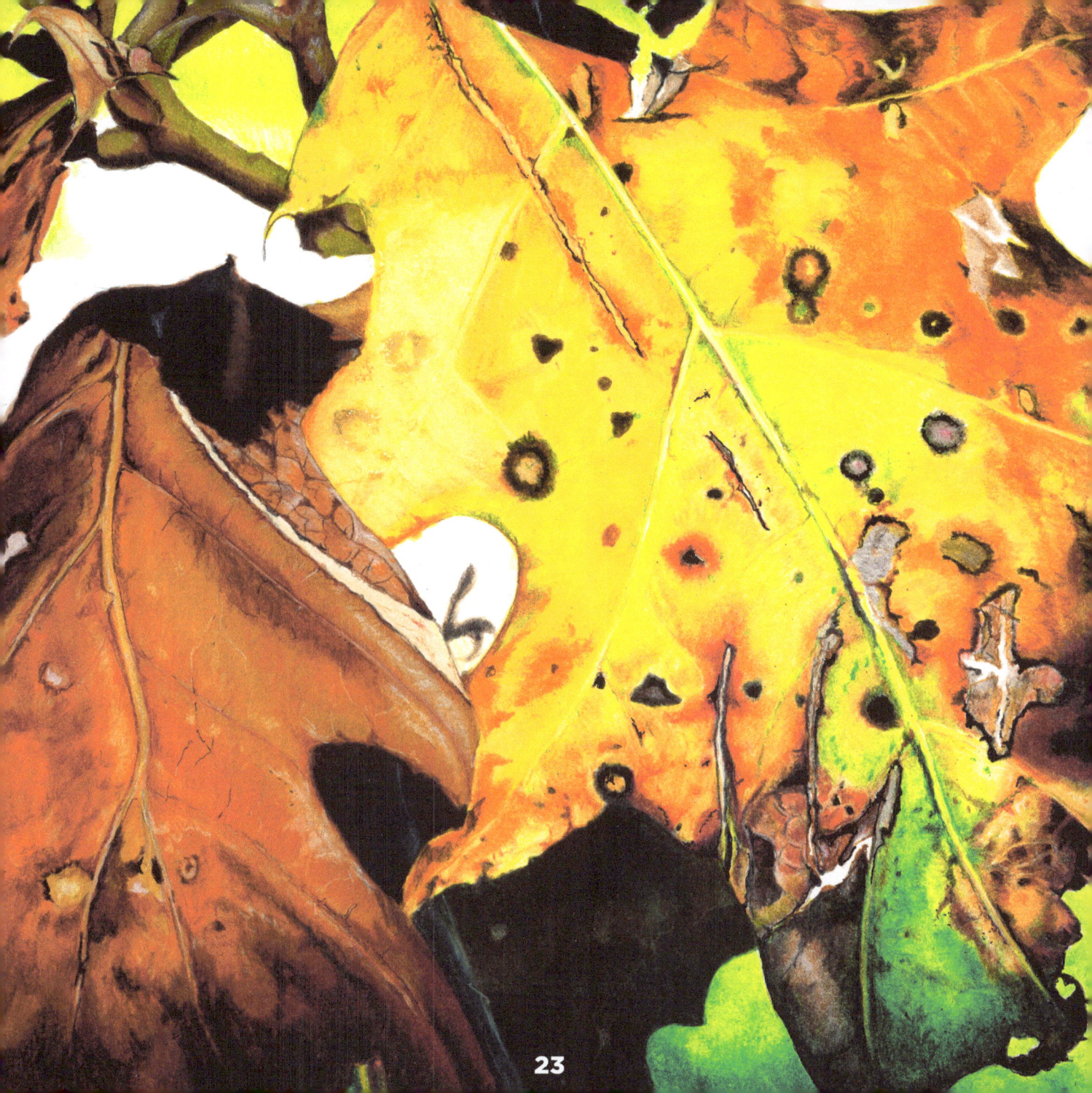

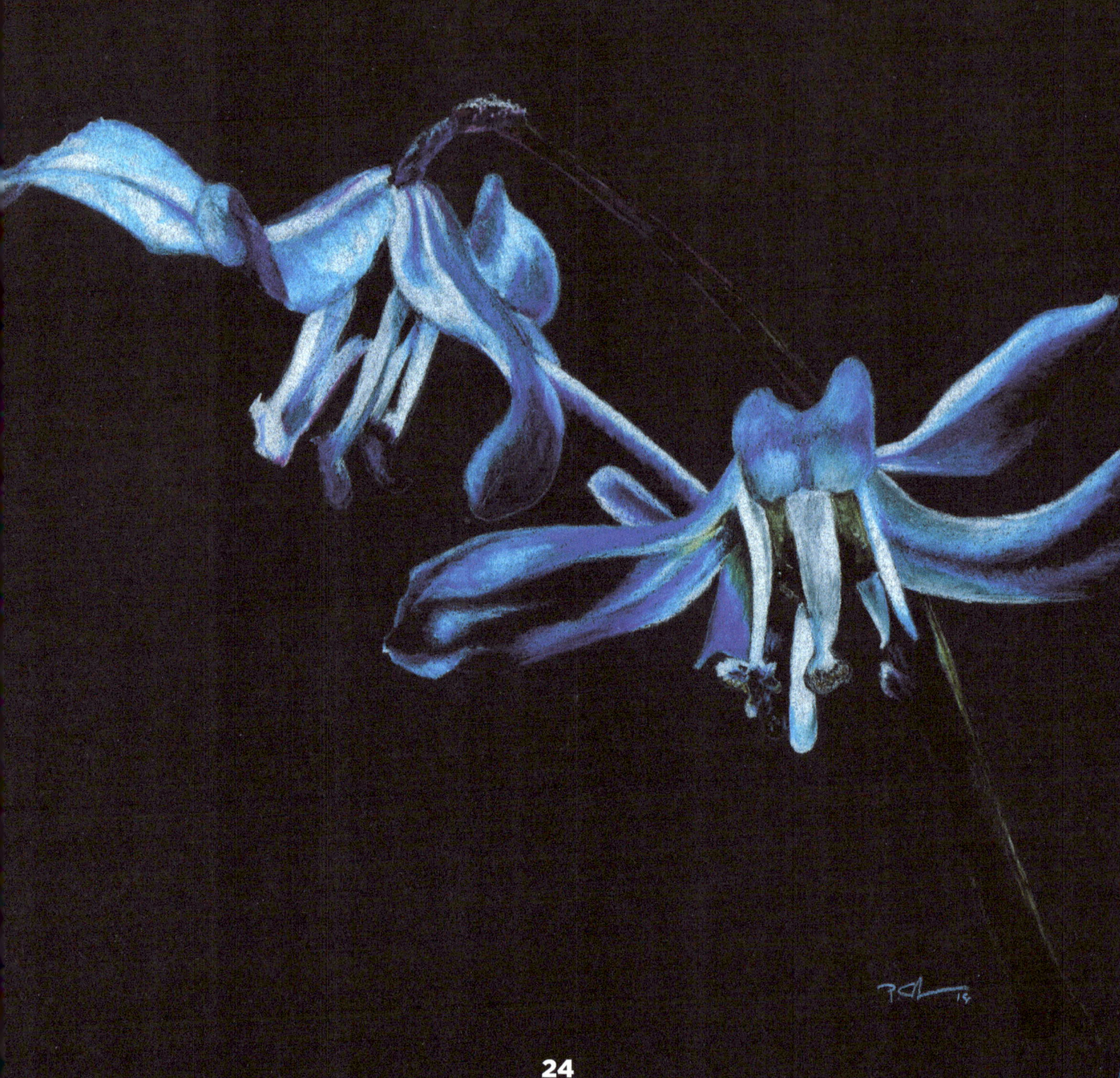

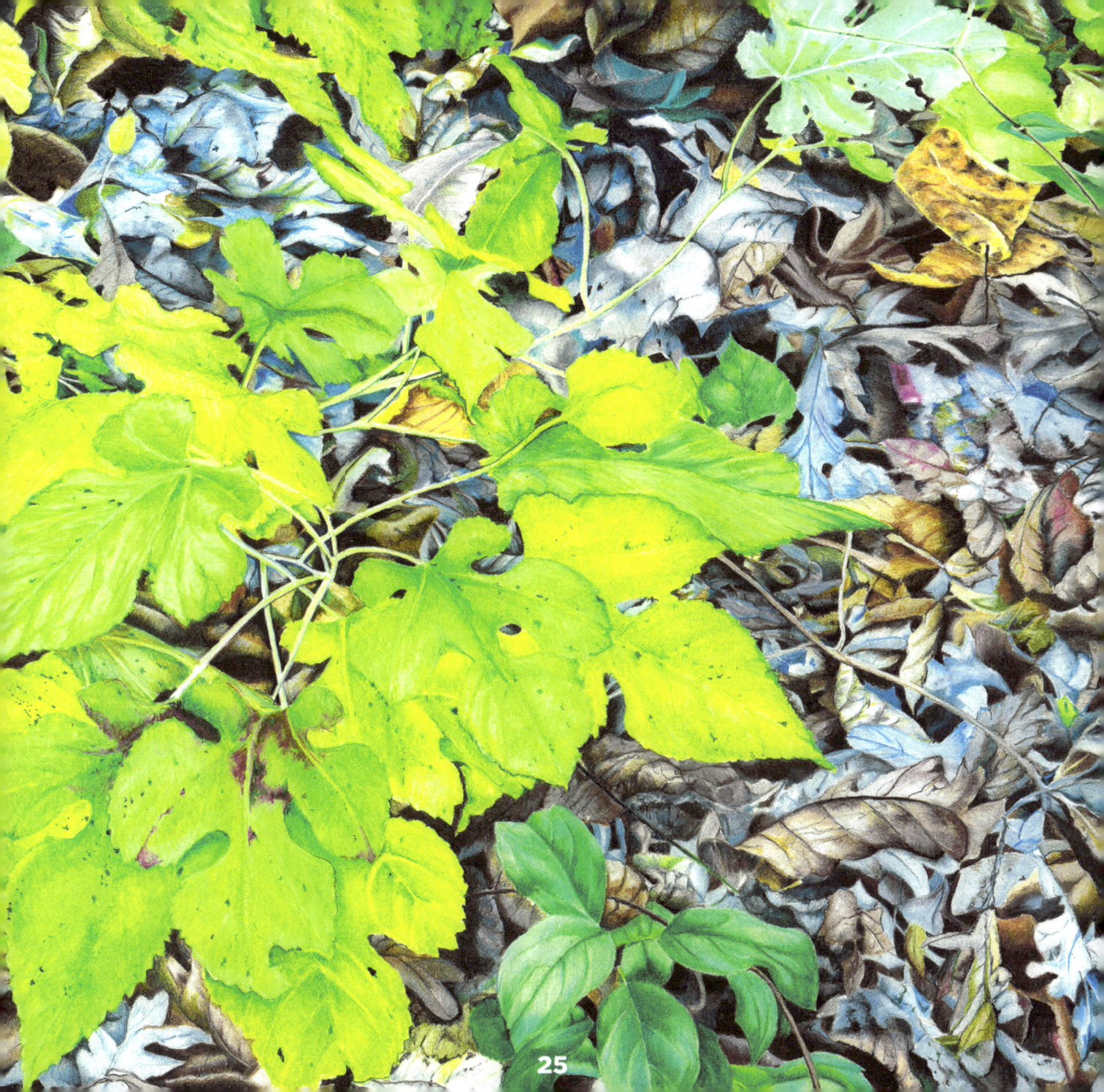

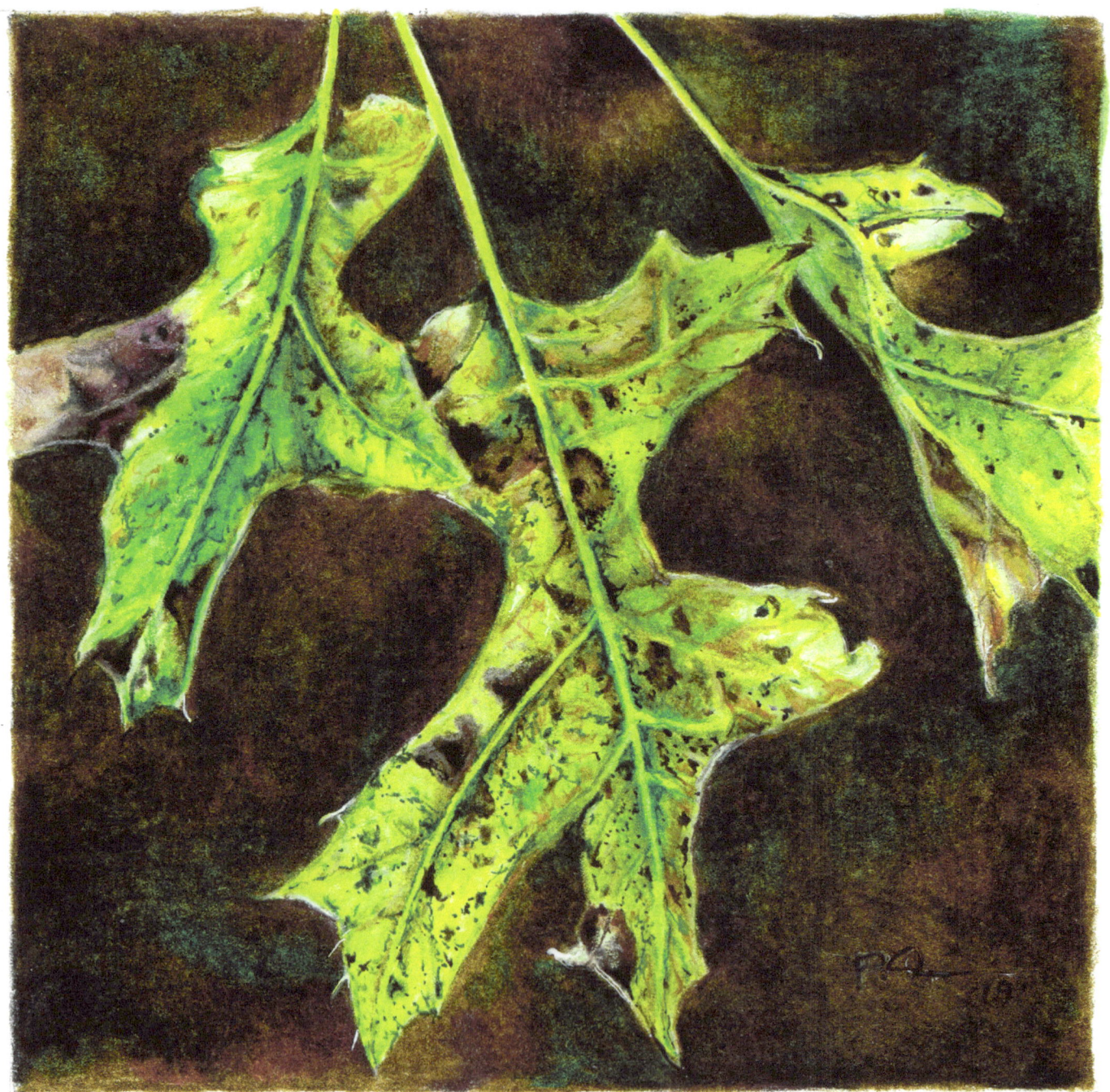

26

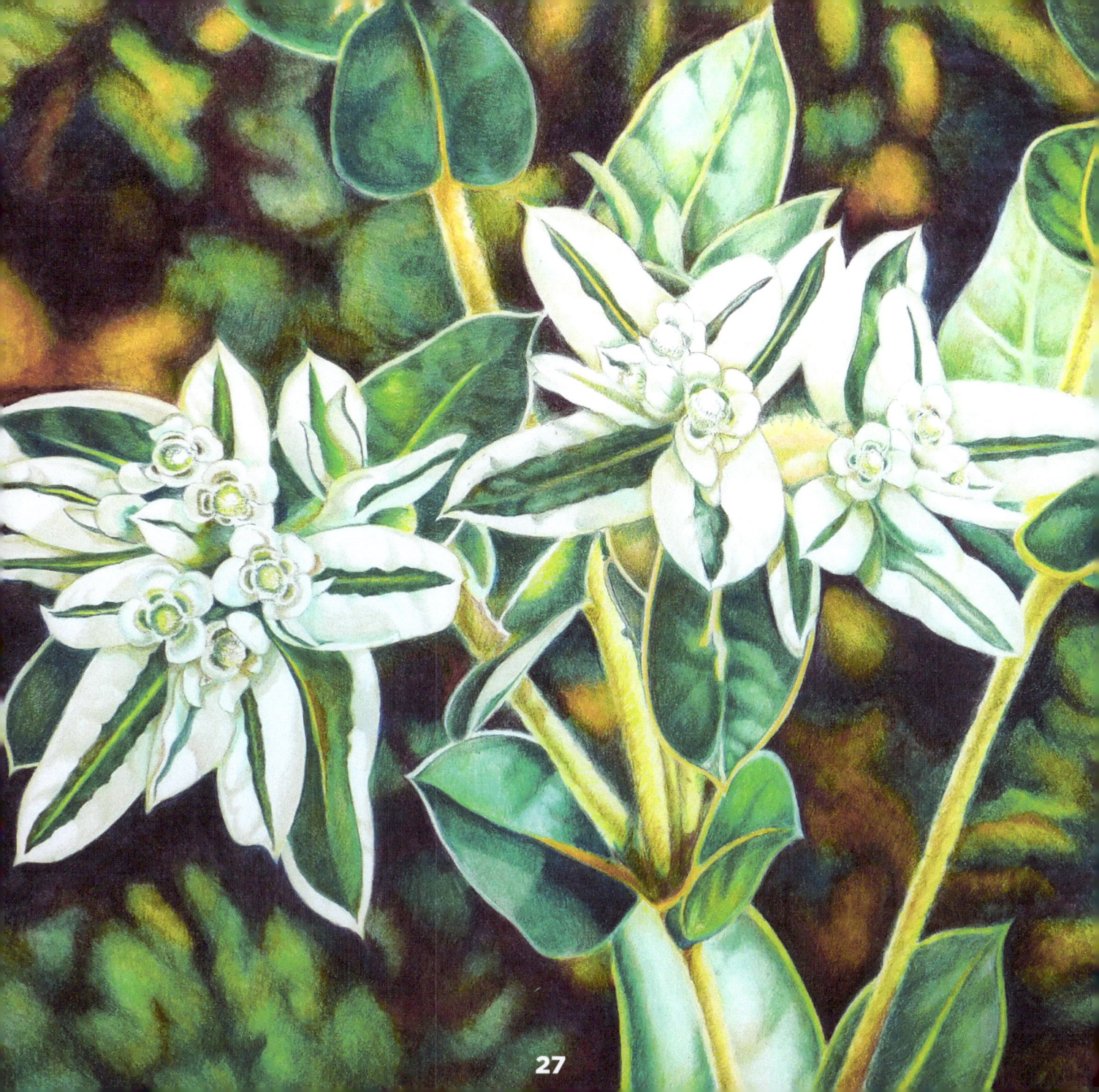

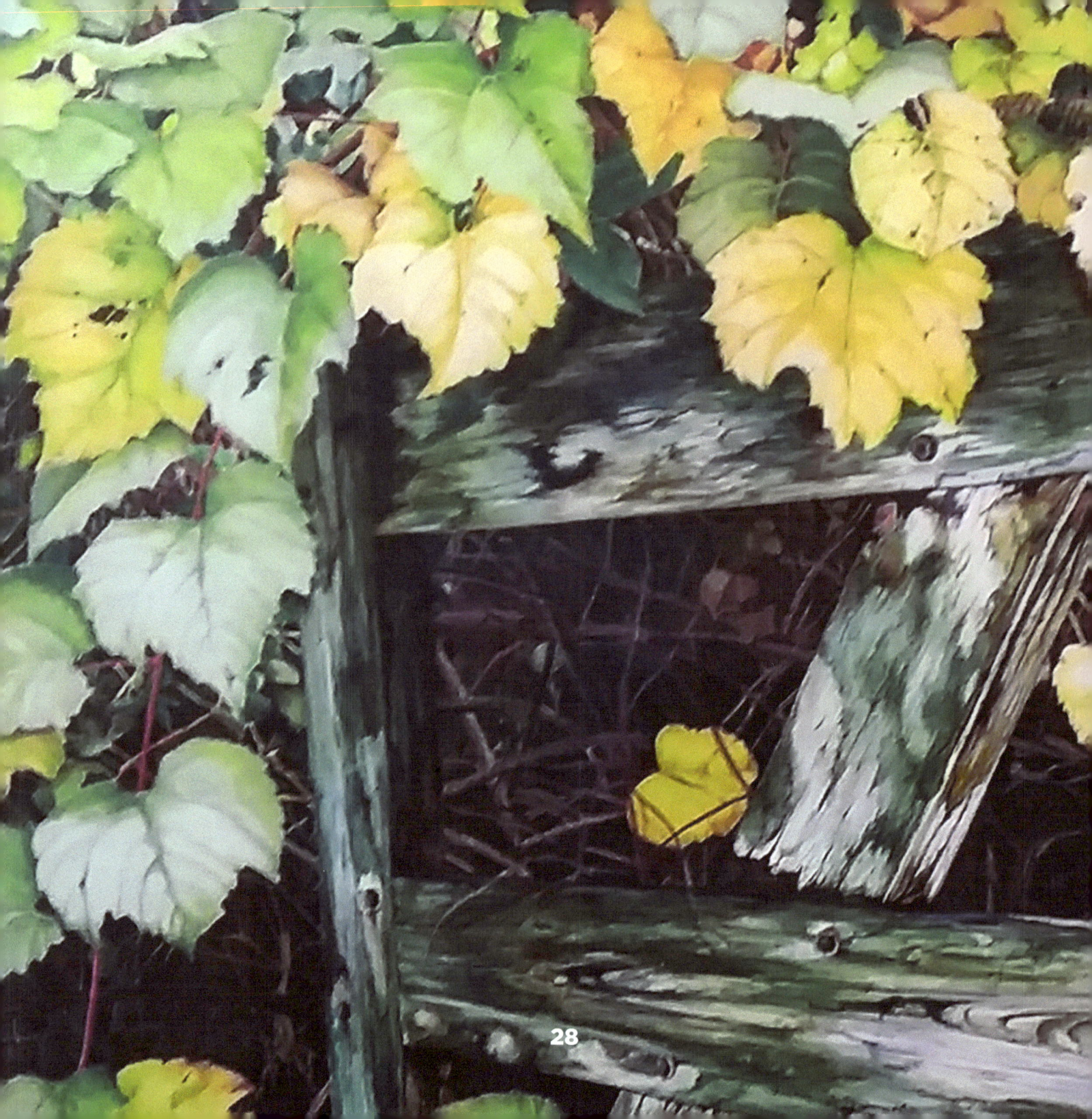

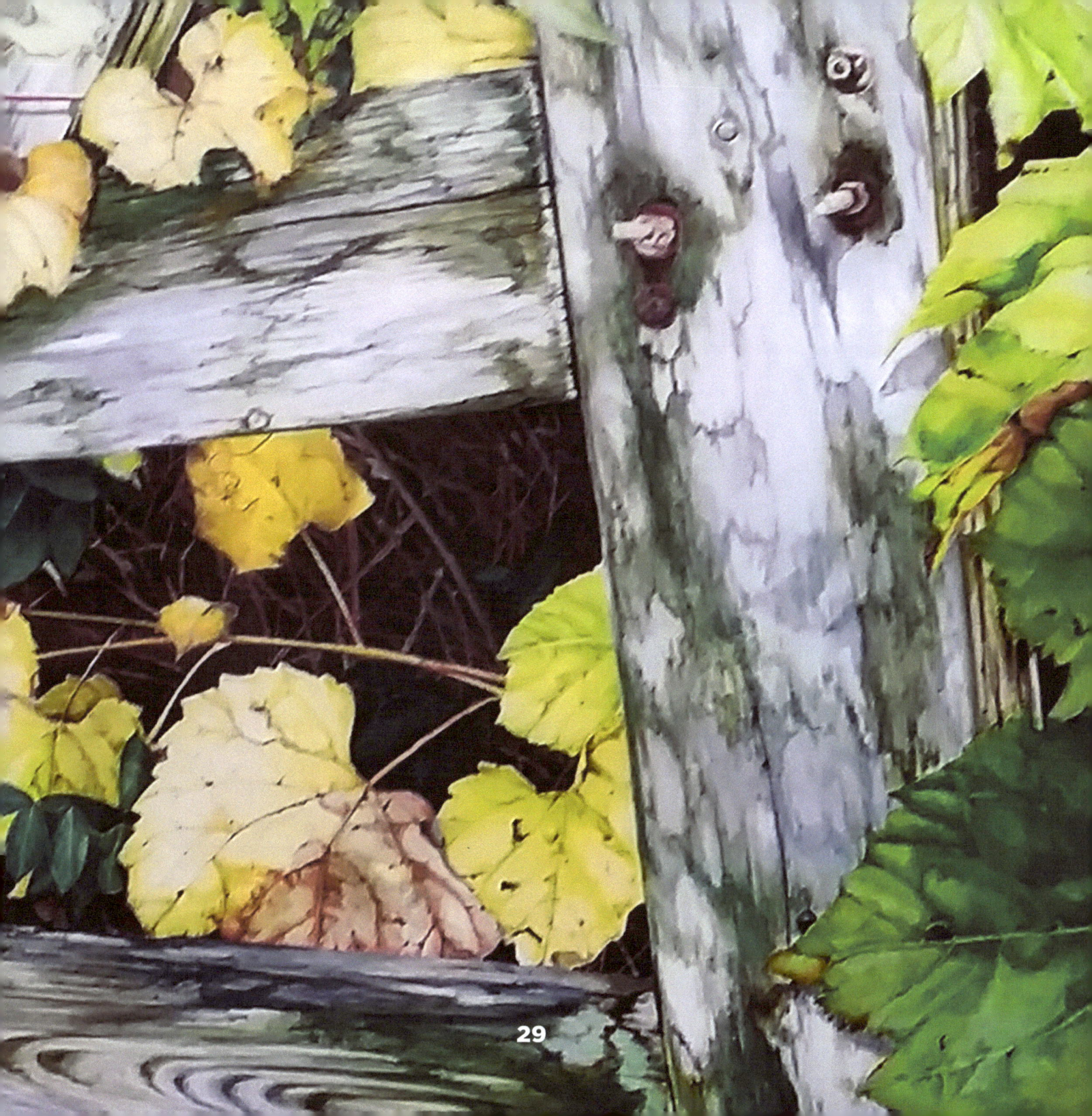

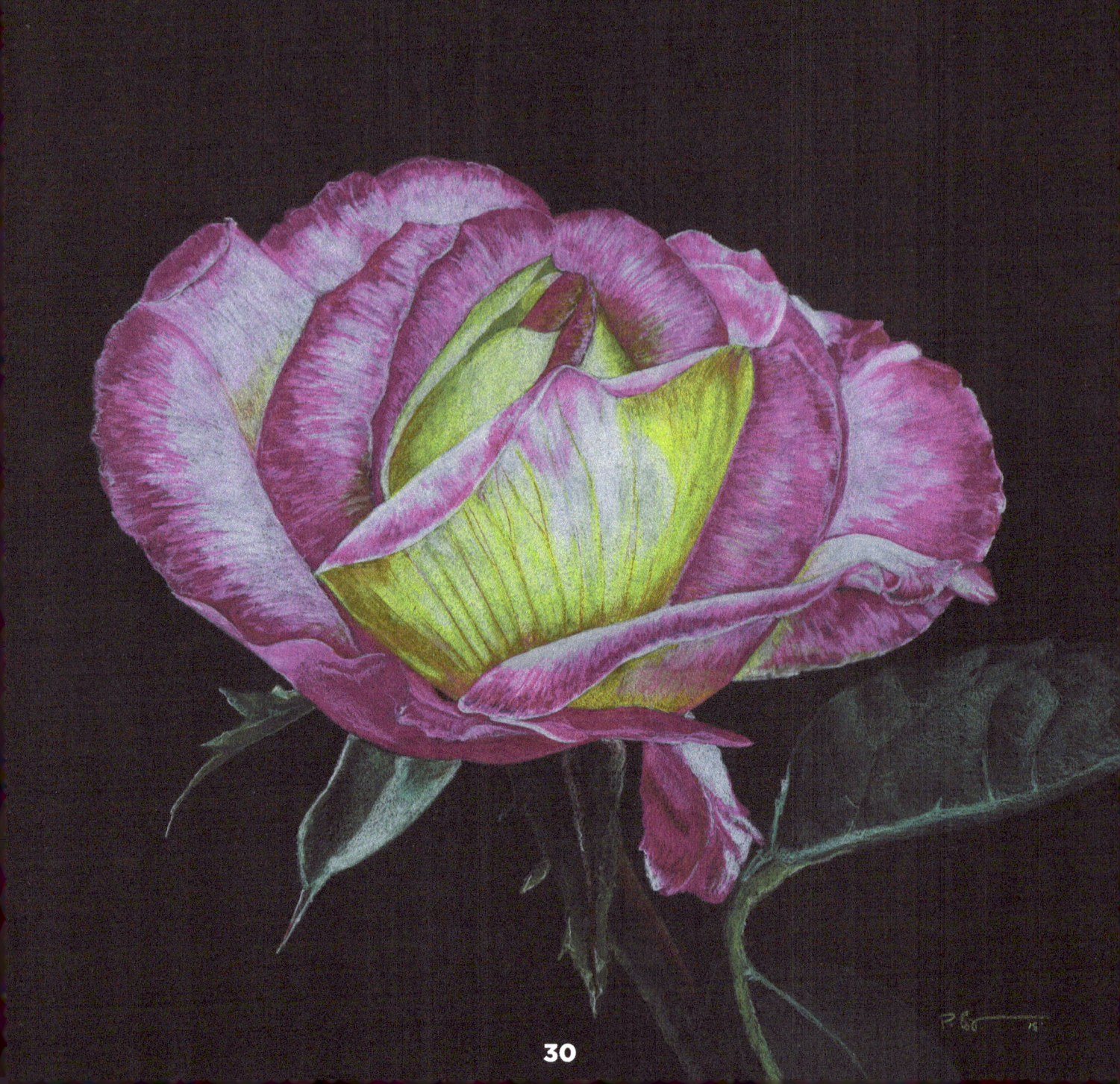

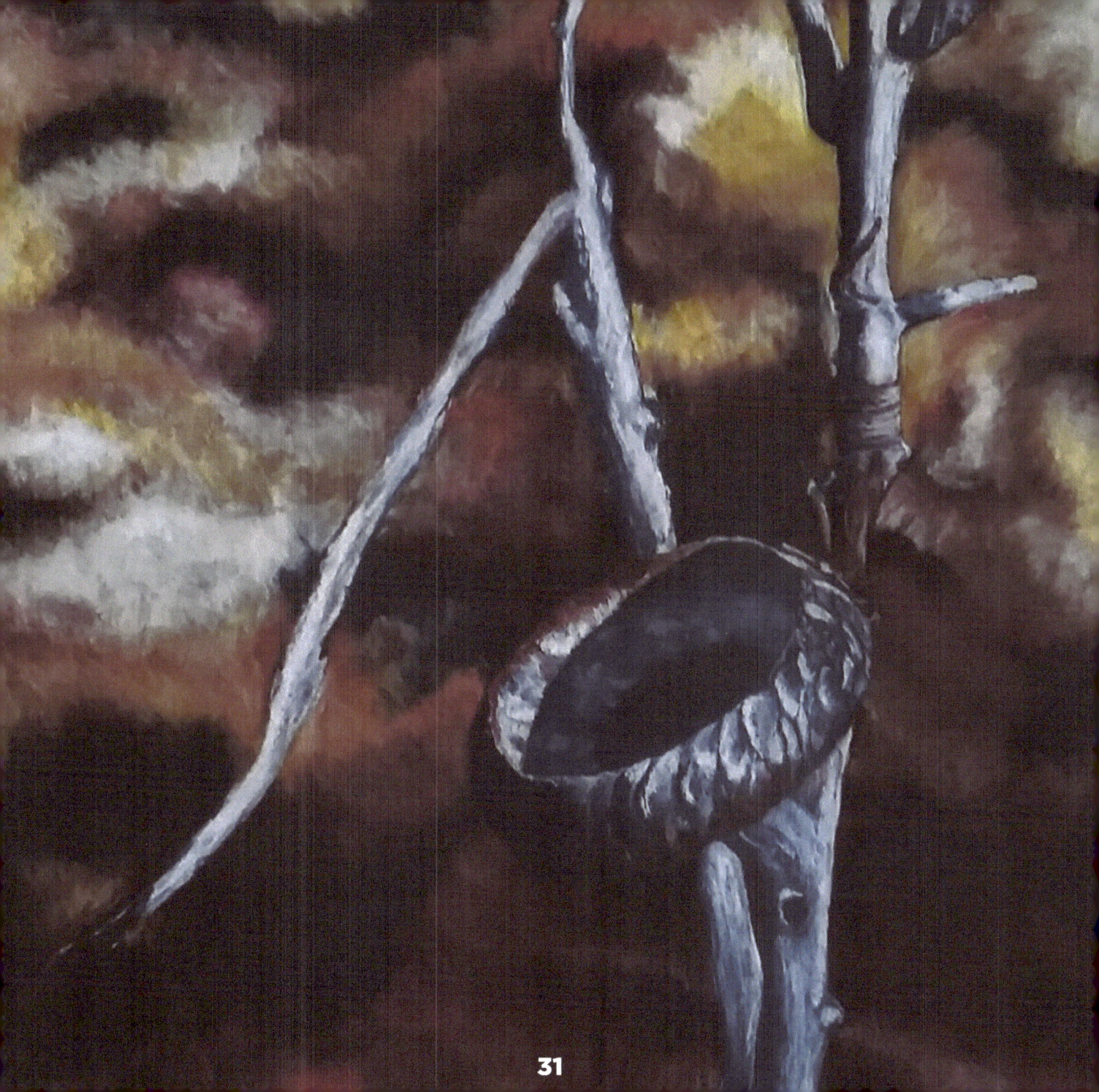

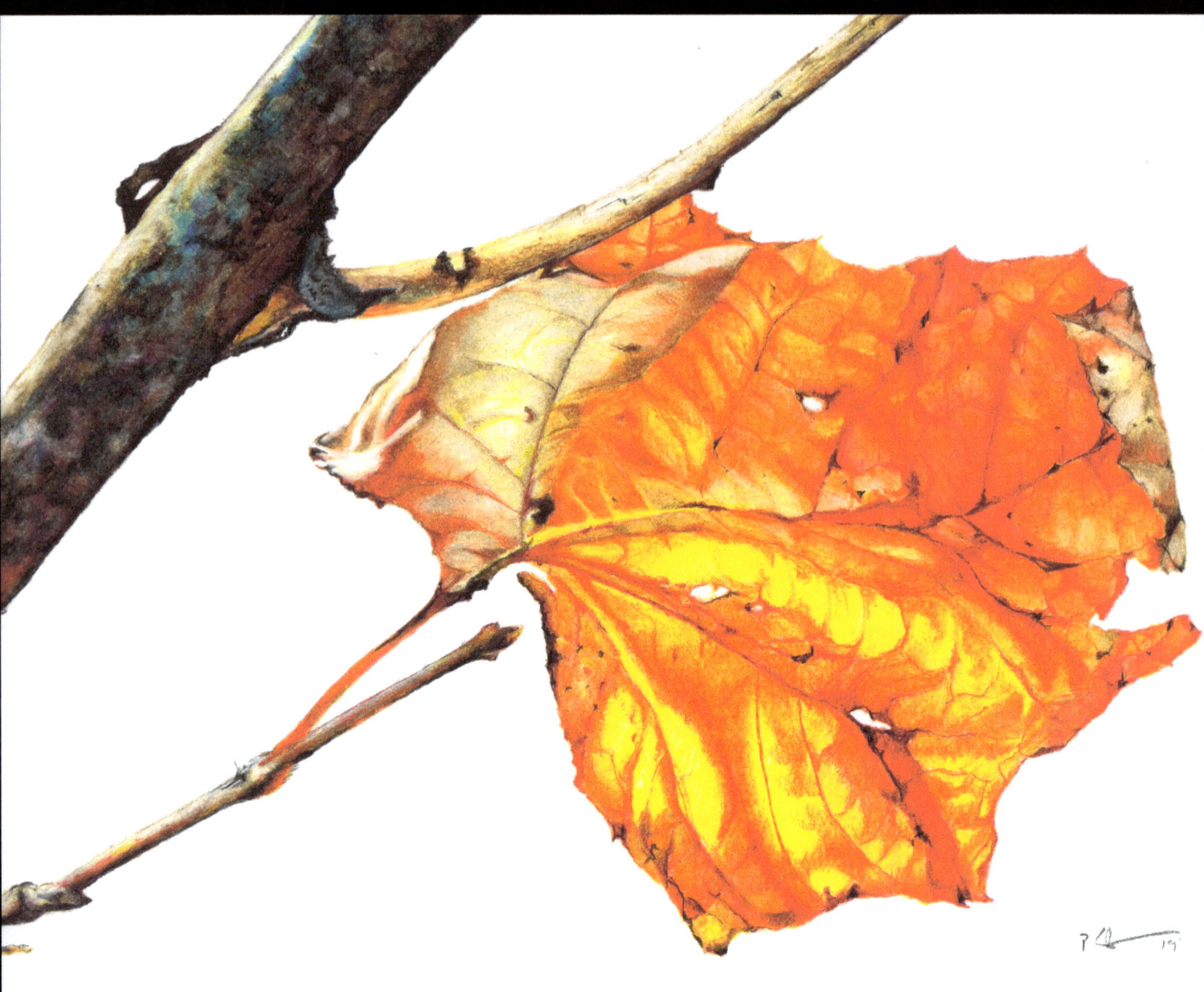

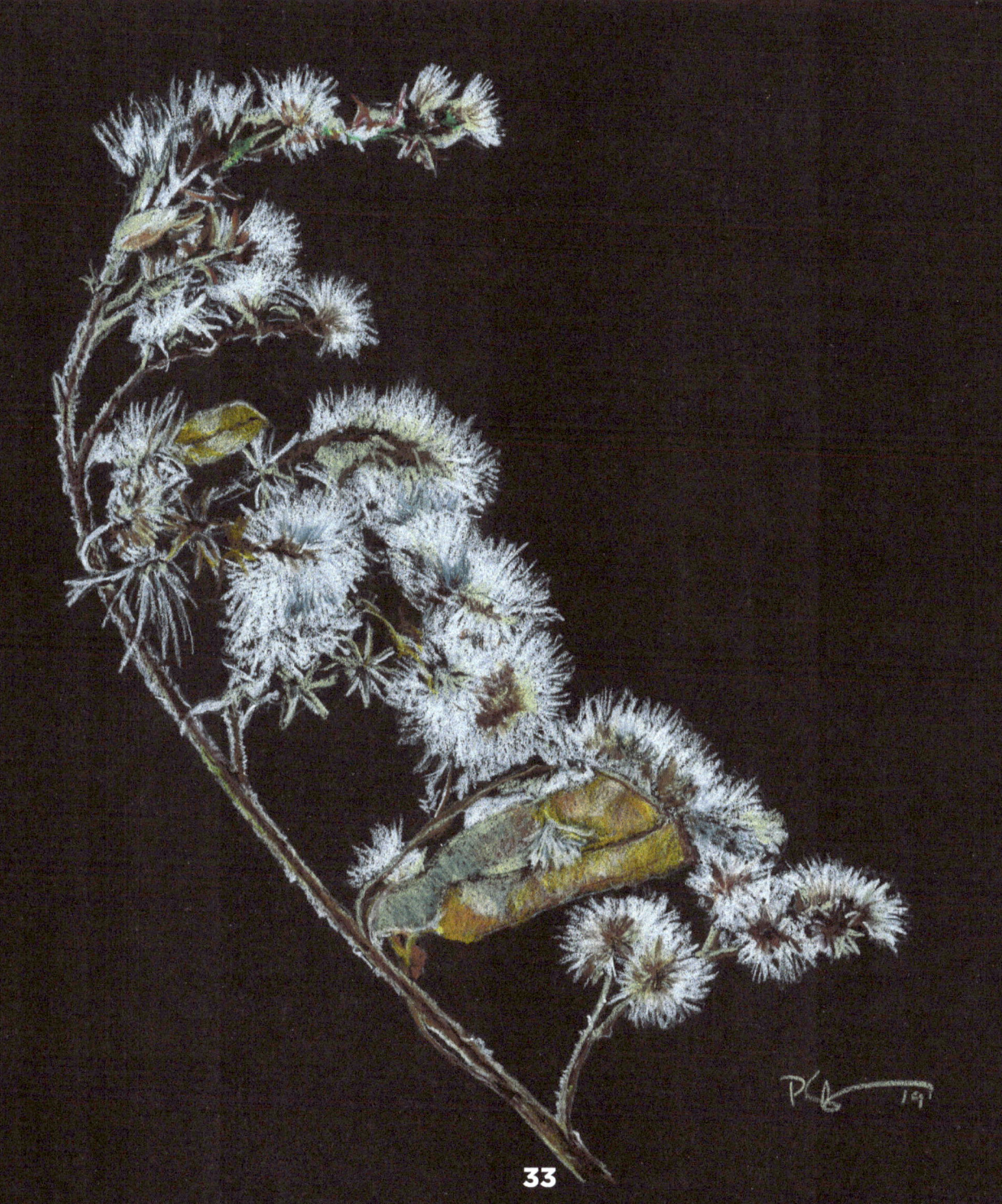

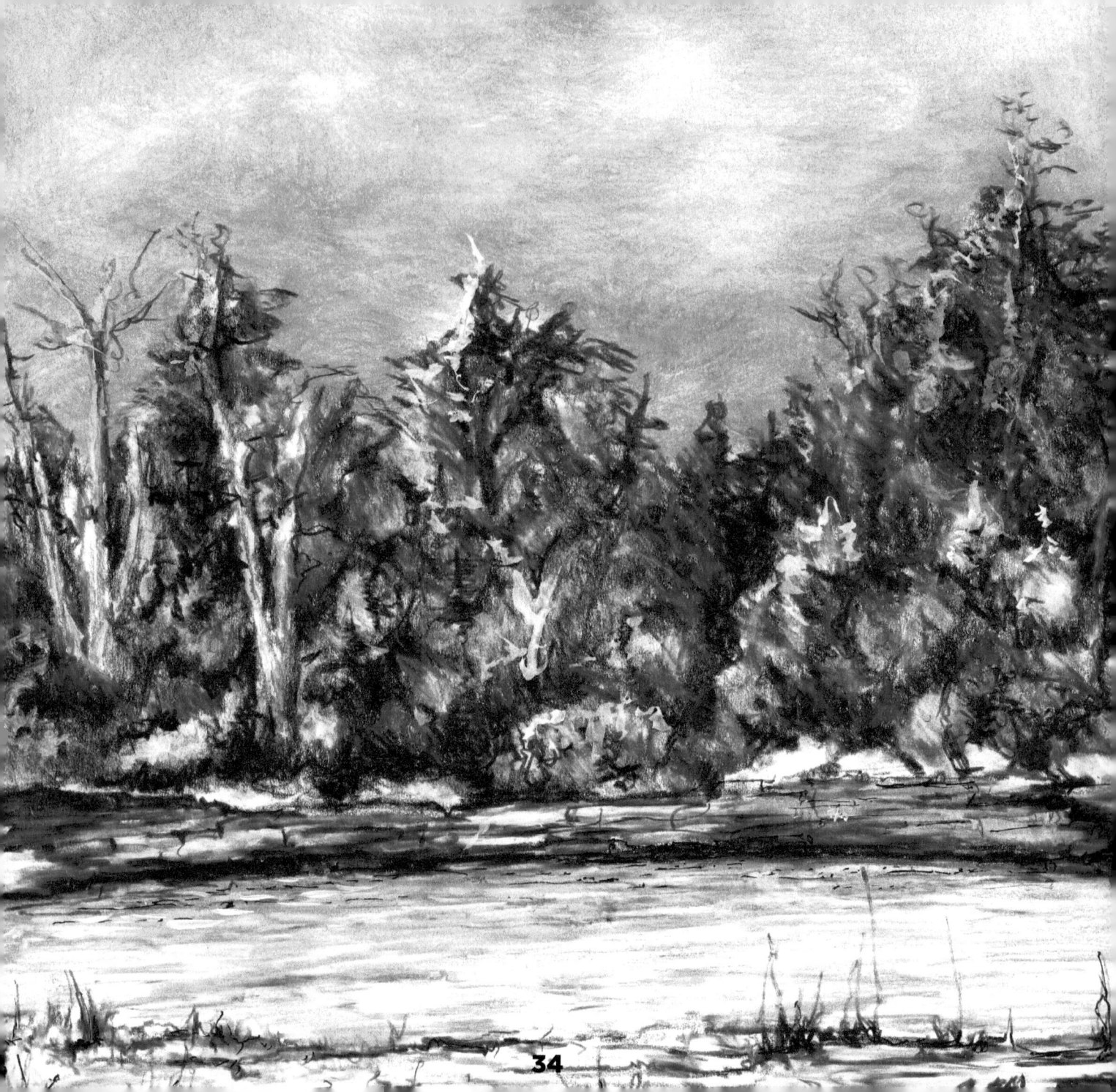

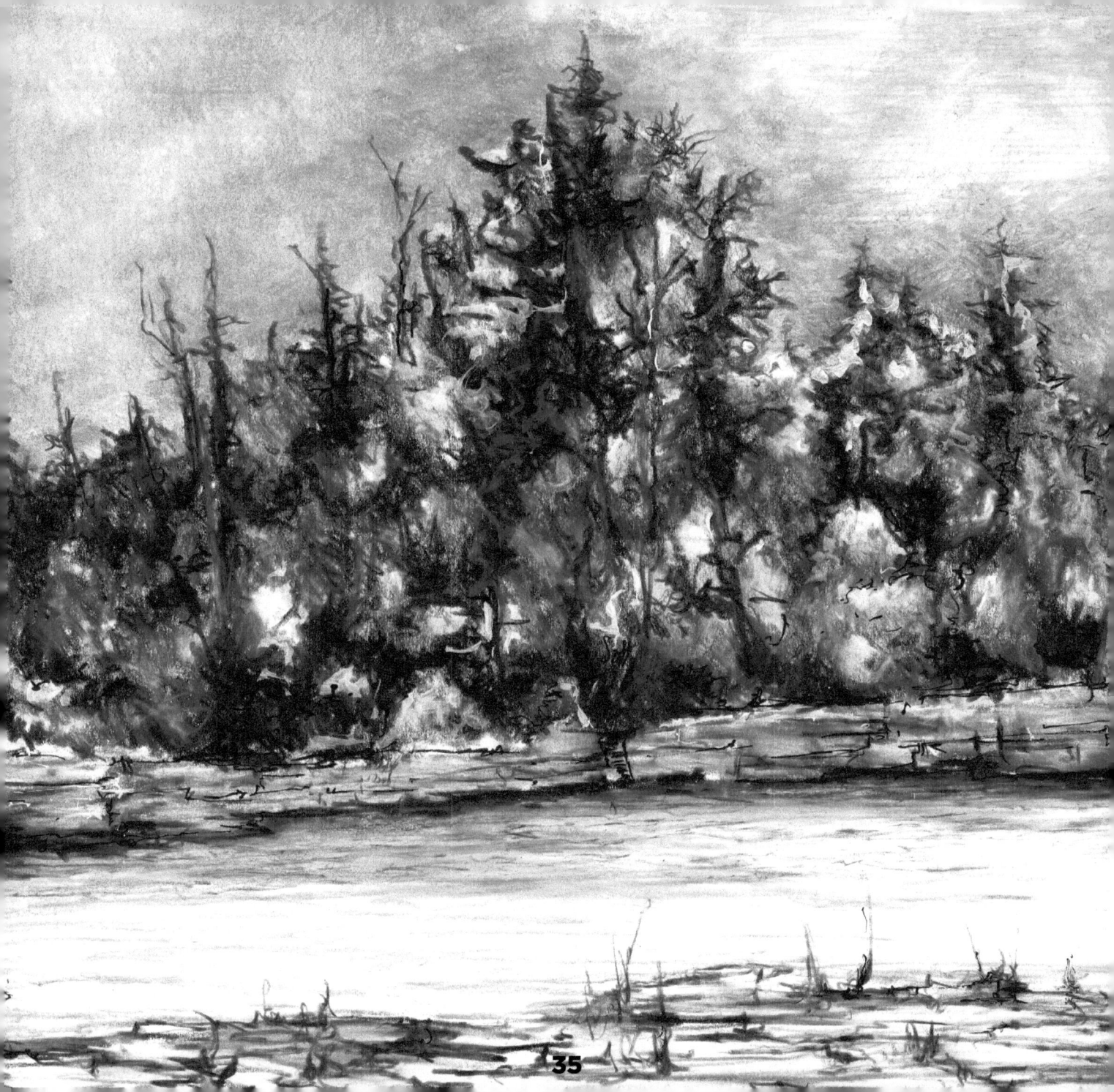

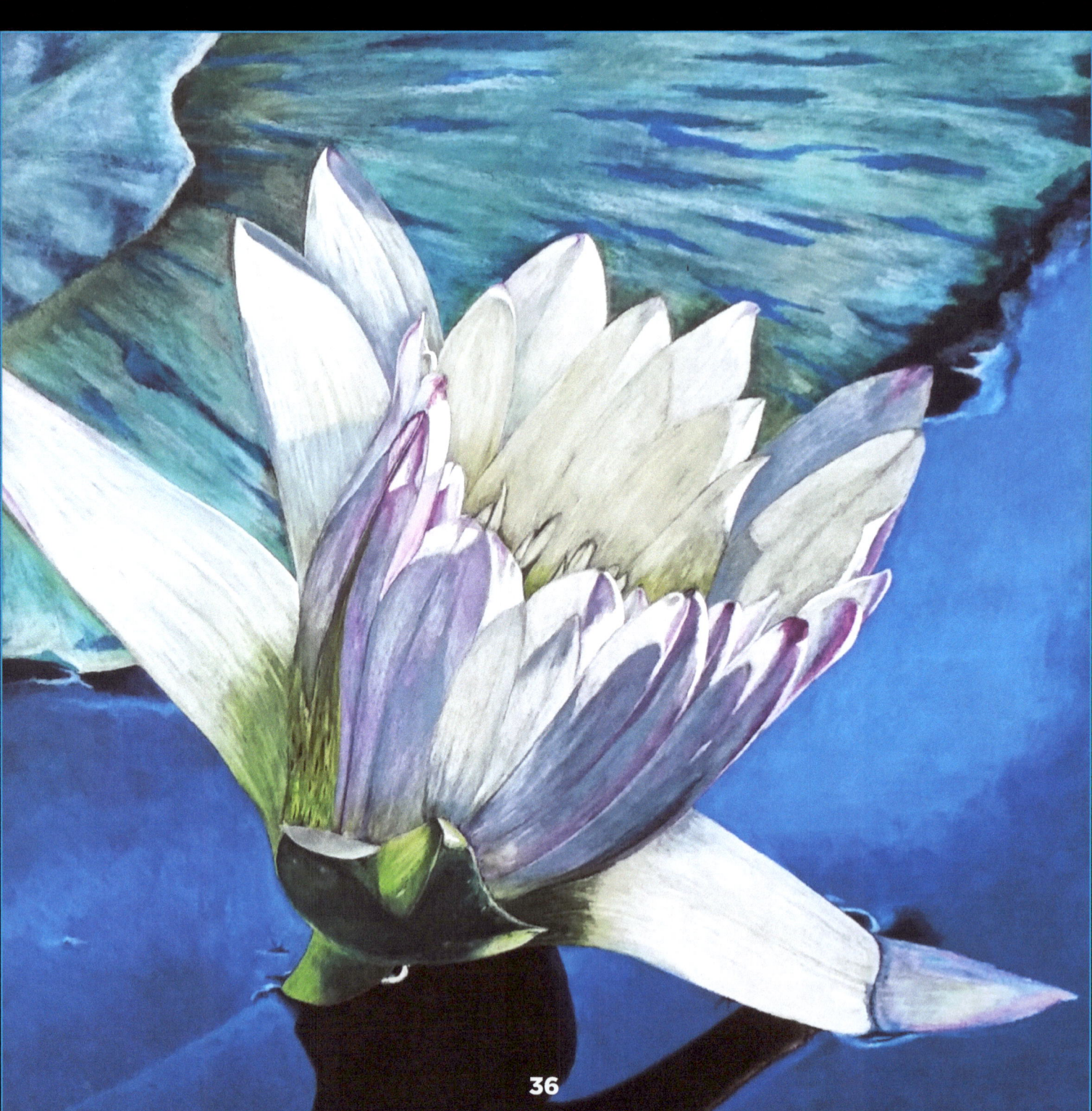

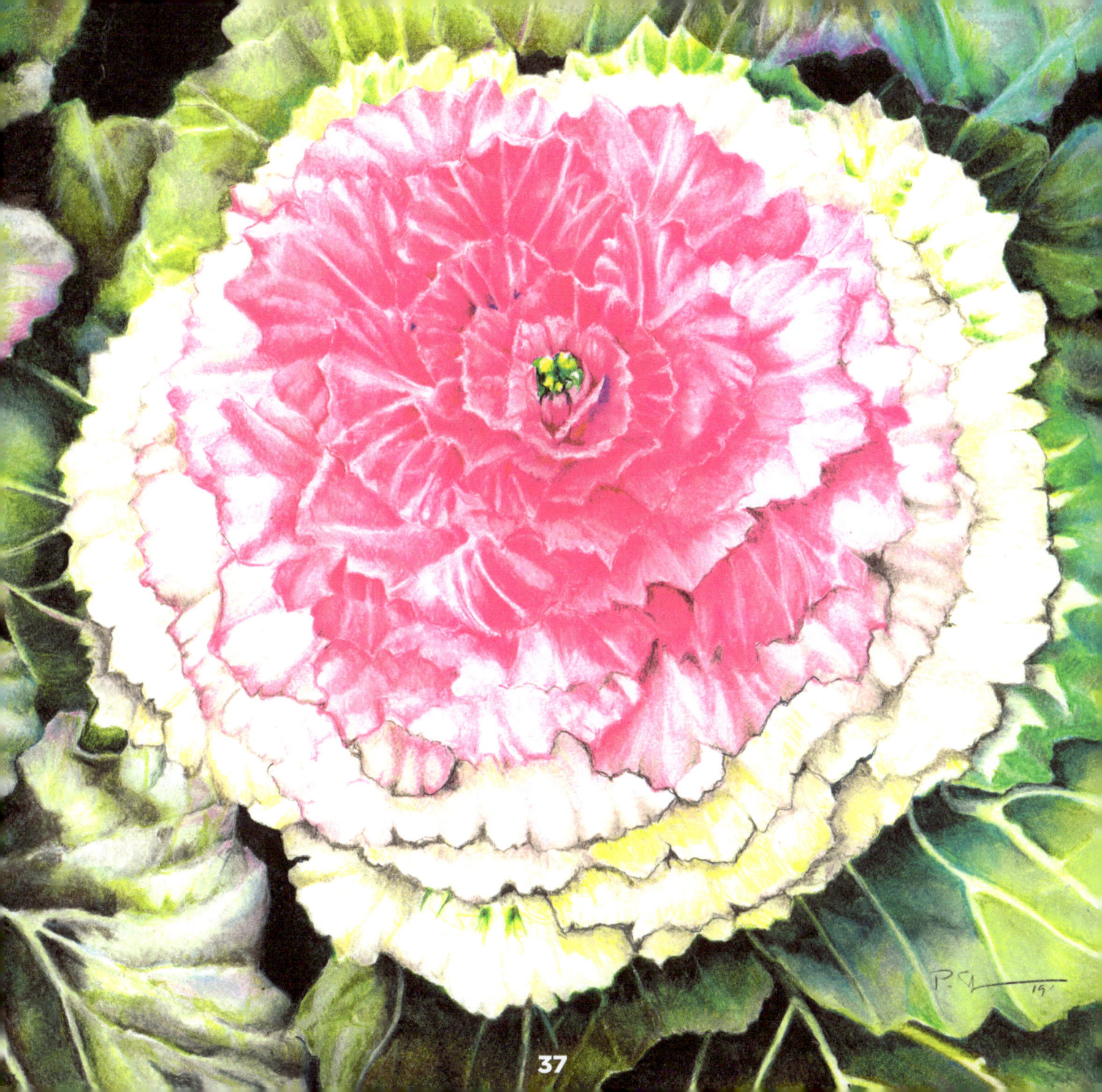

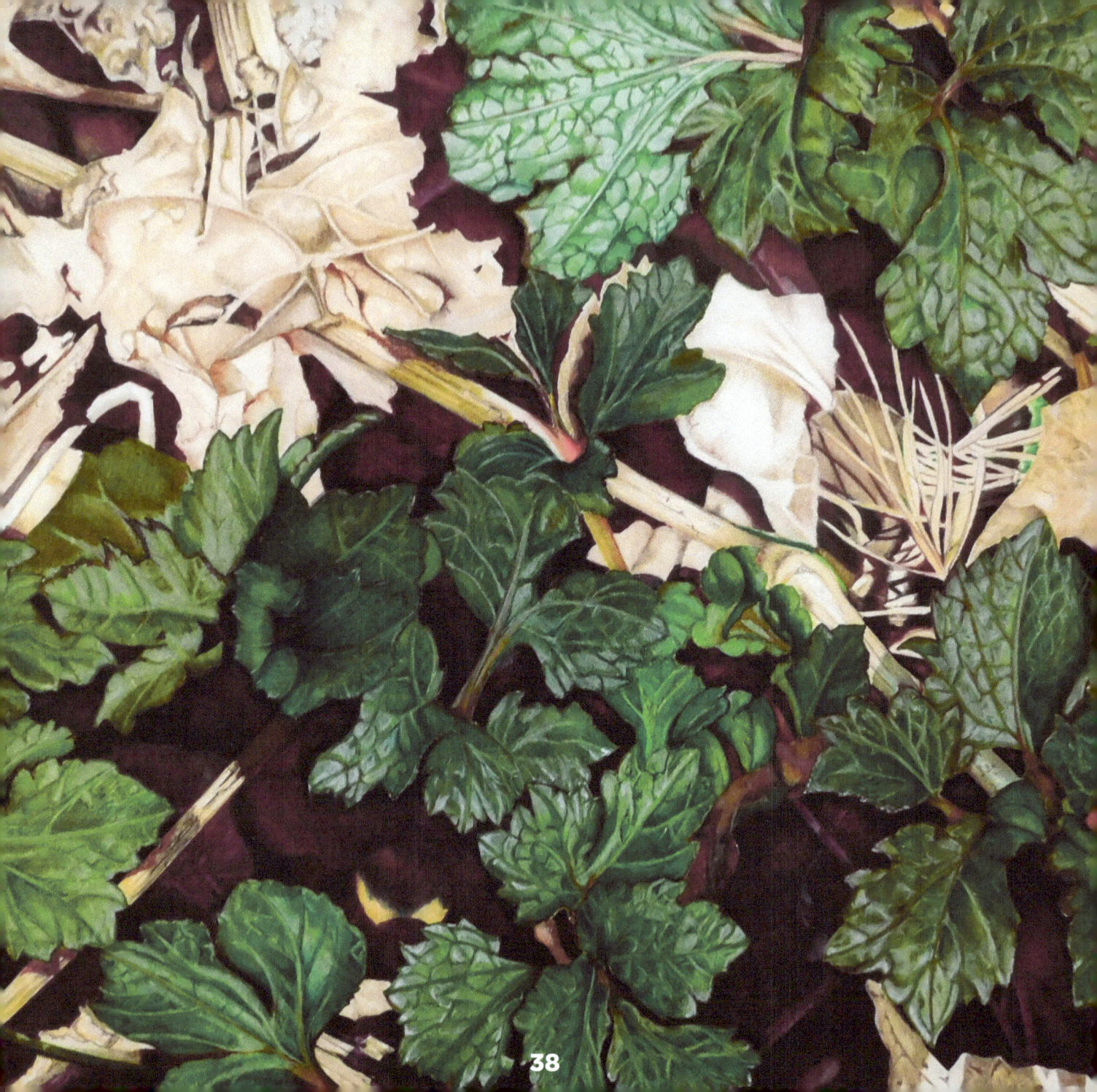

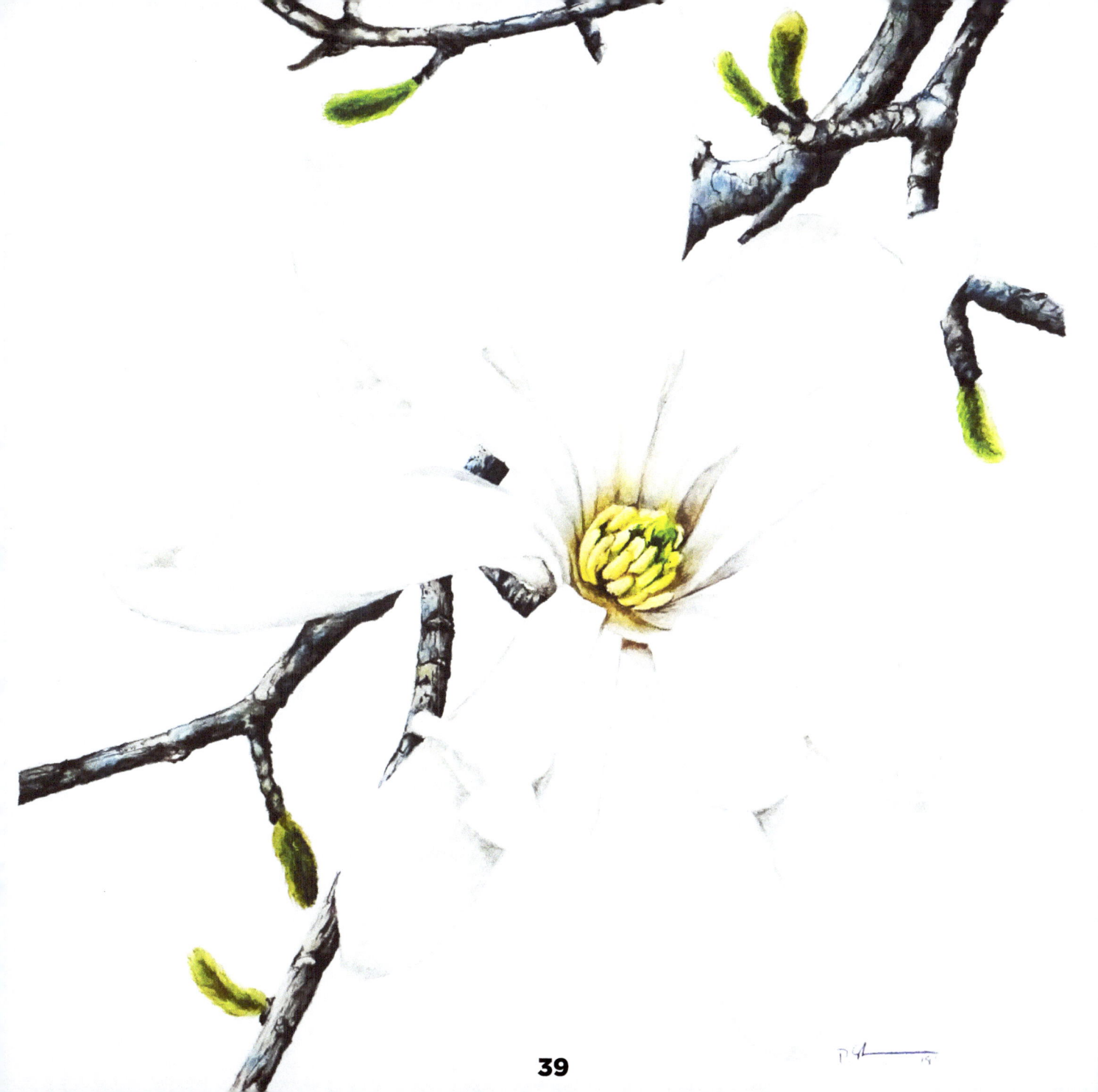

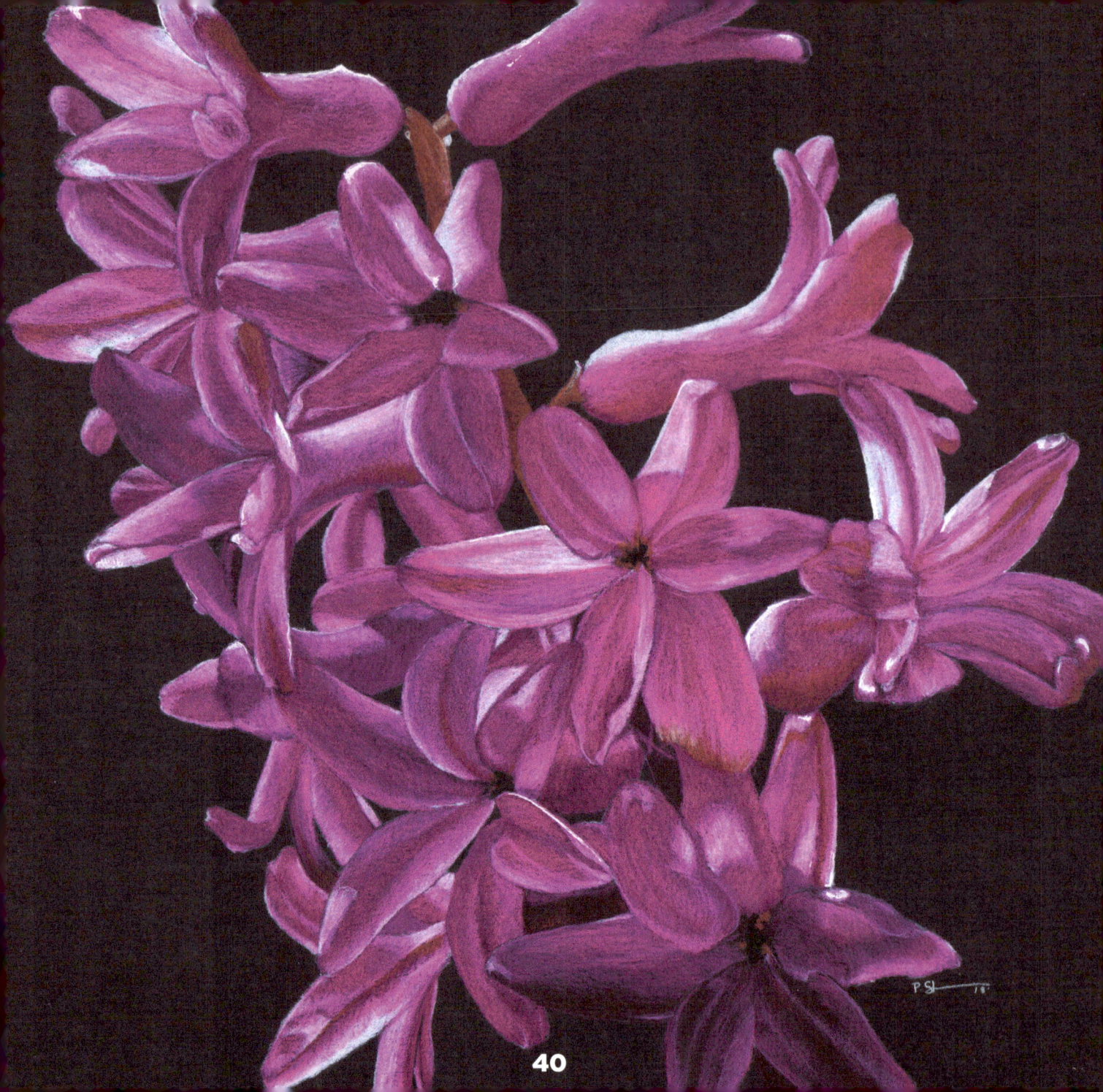

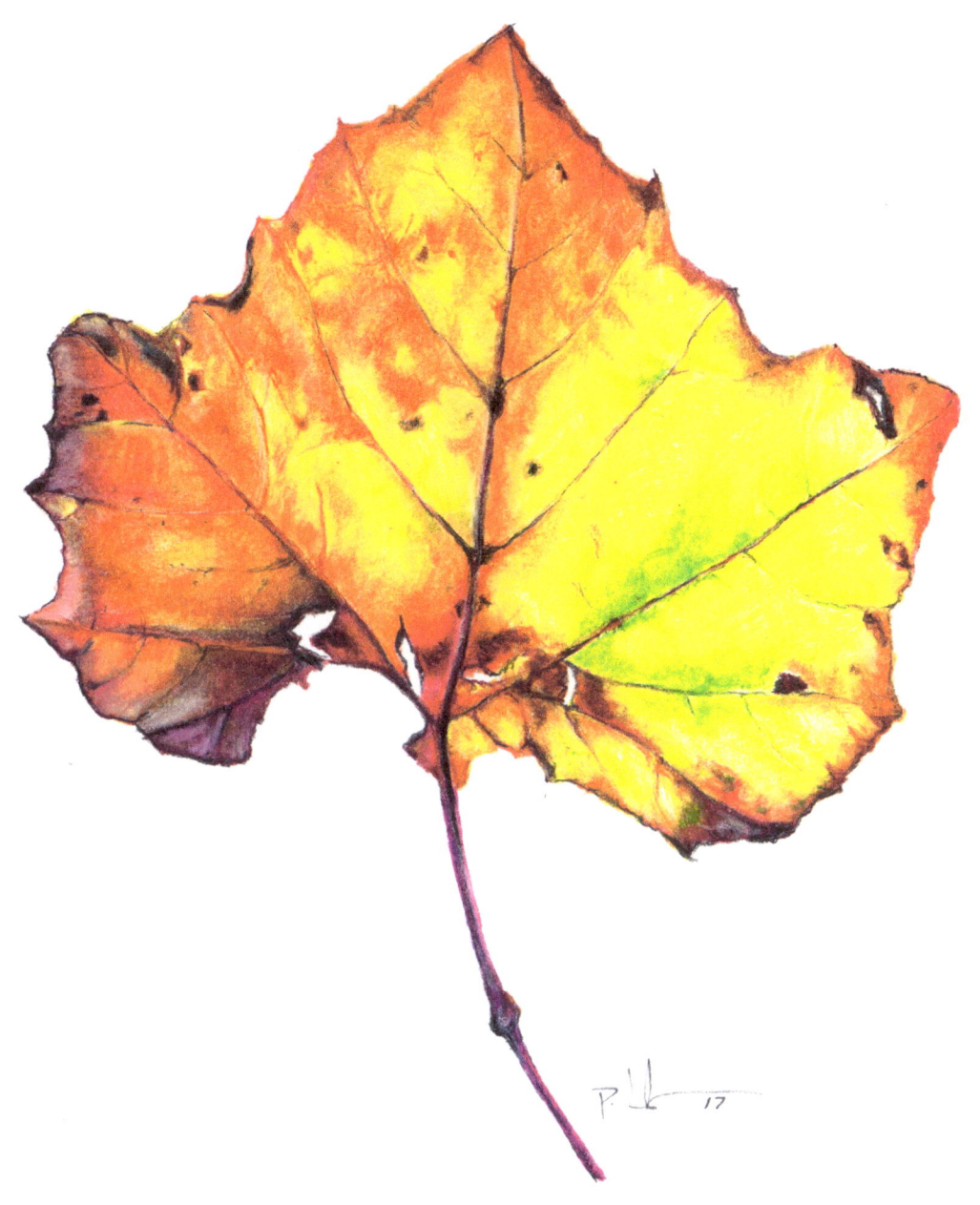

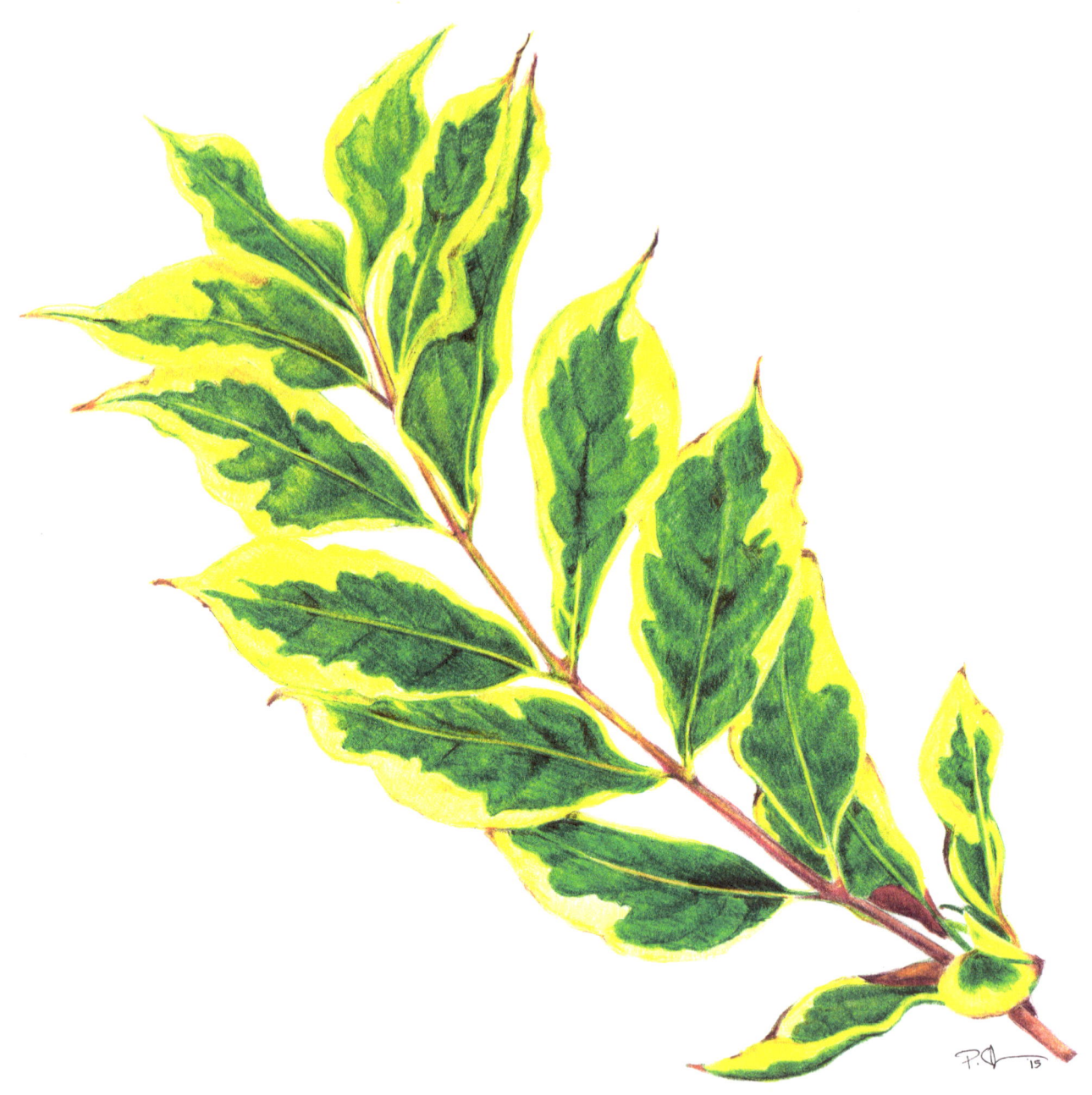

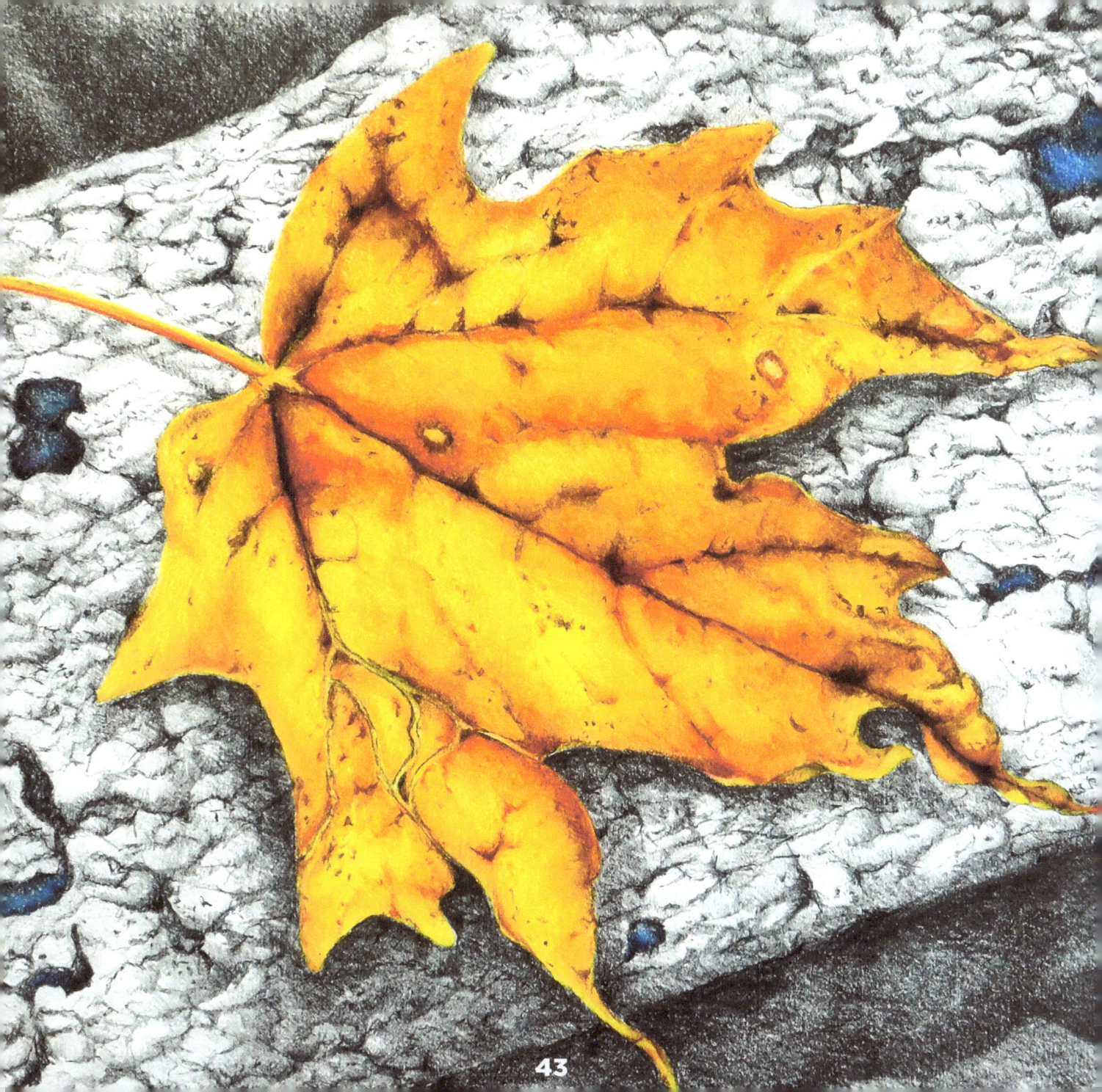

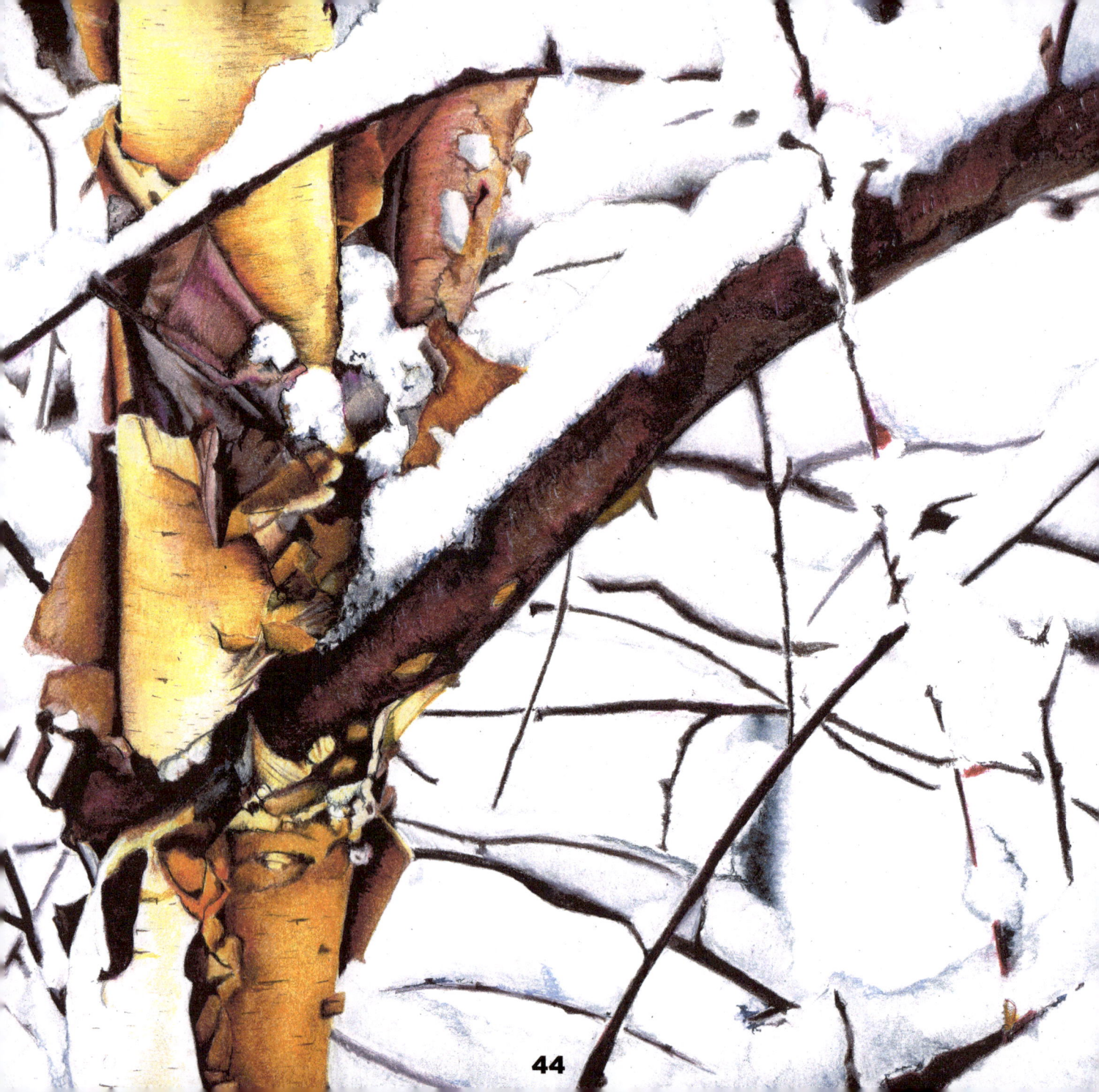

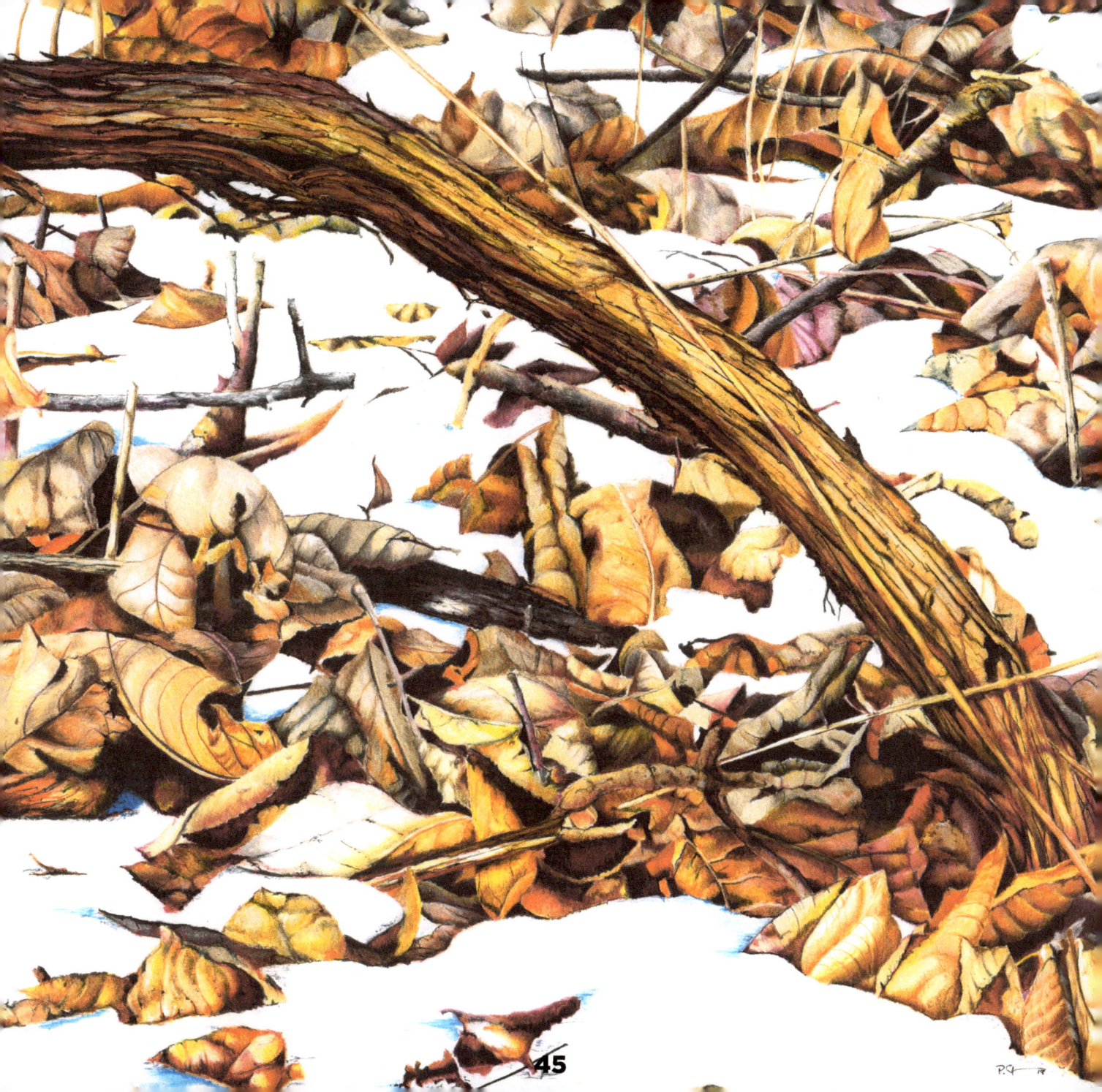

45

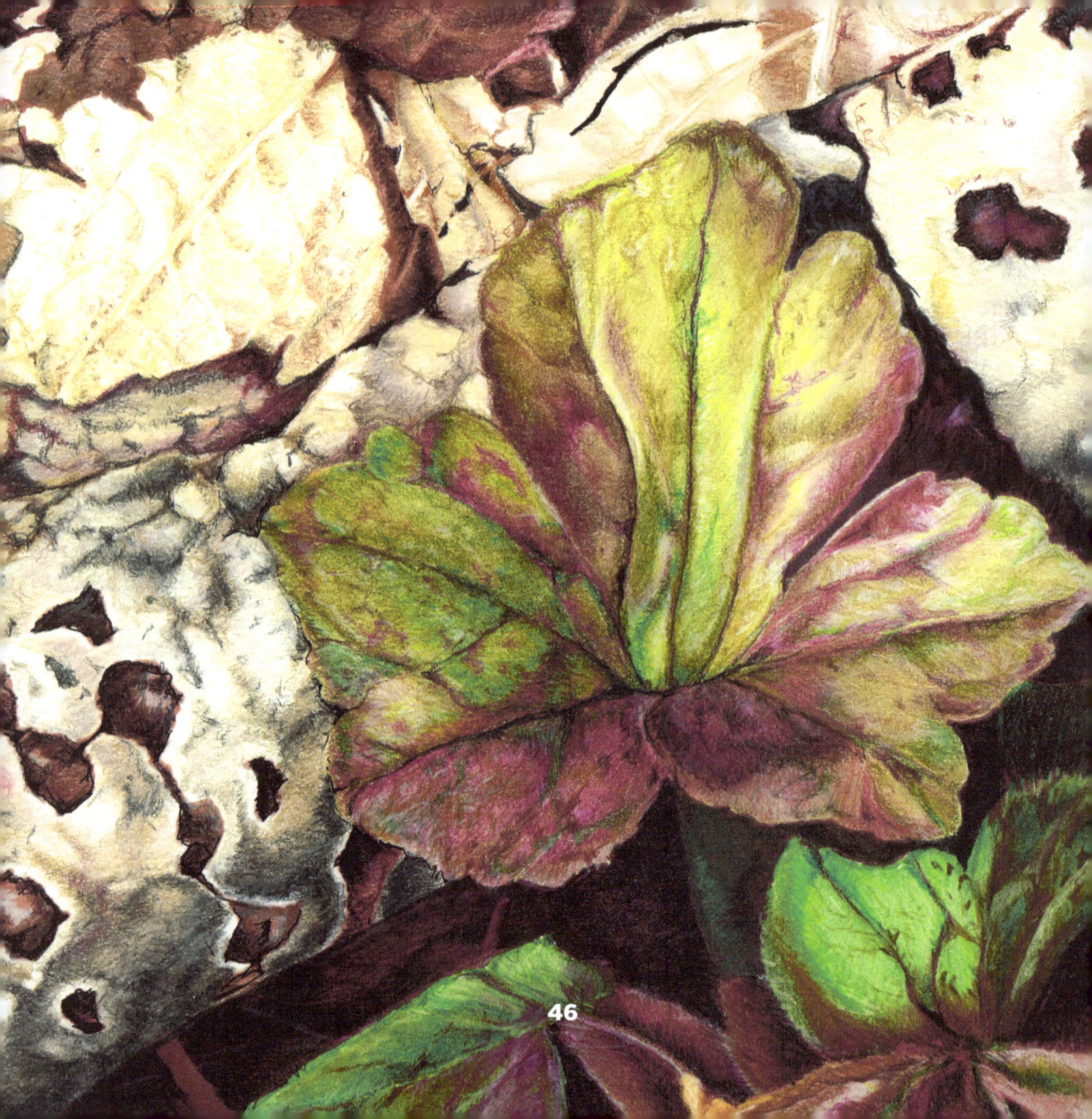

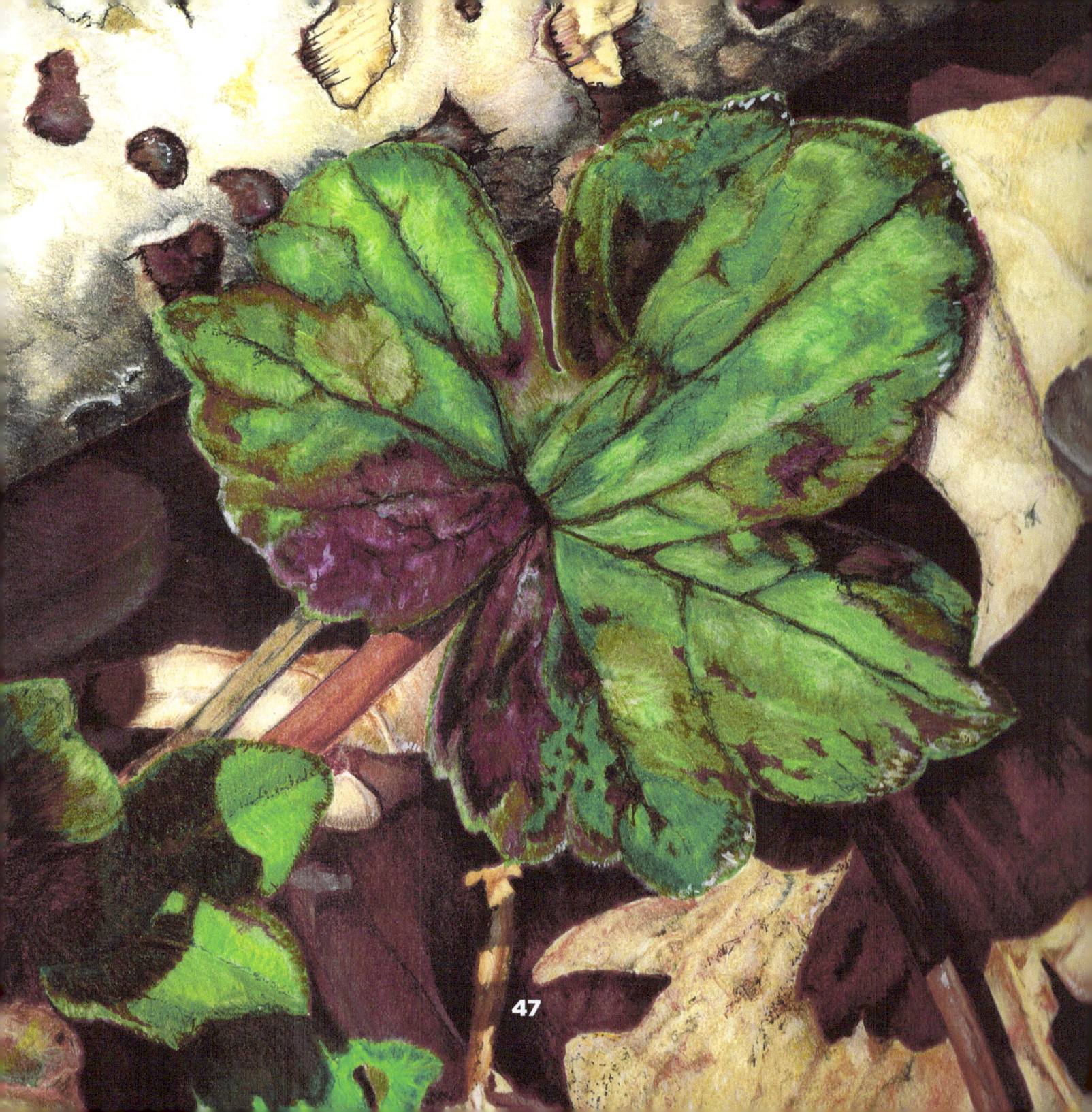

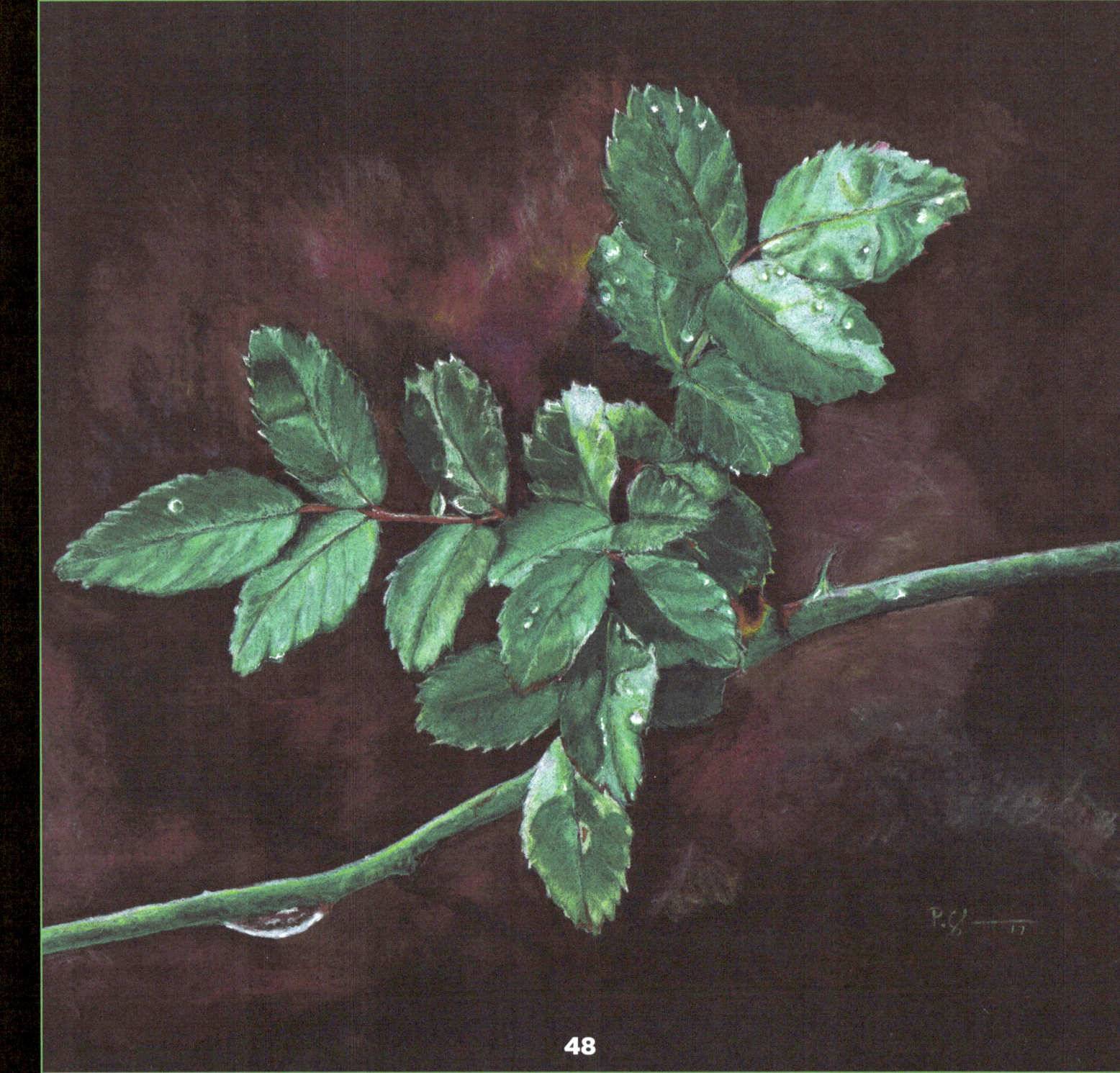

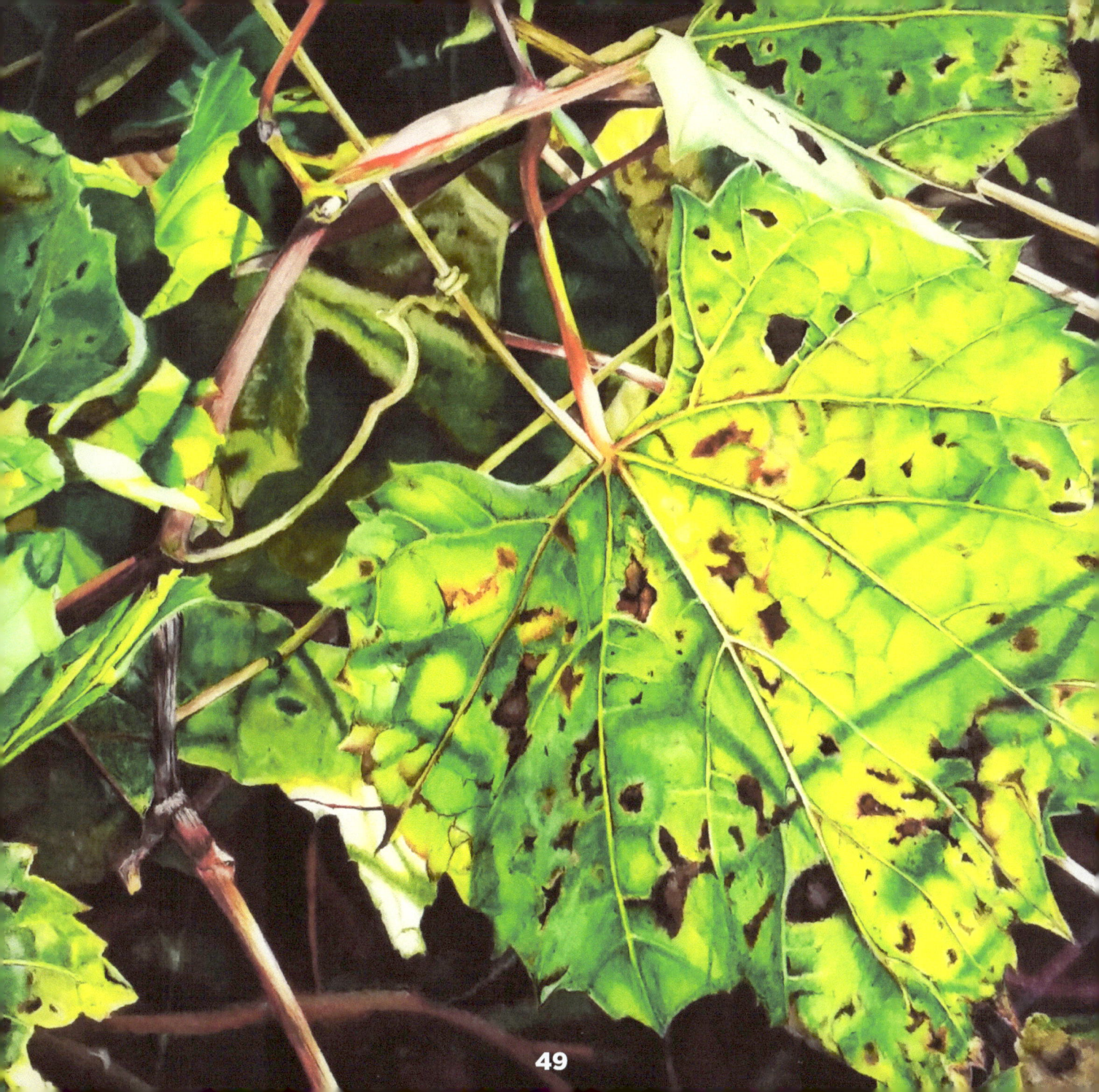

LIST OF IMAGES

*some of the images shown have been cropped to fit the format of this book.

A COMPLETE LISTING OF ALL MY ART
CAN BE SEEN AT PSCHORNSTUDIO.COM

DRAWING TIPS
in no particular order.

TIP - Get the best pencils you can afford, even if it is a few colors, it will make a difference.

TIP - Draw small, keep your strokes no longer than 1/8th of inch.

TIP - All paper has a texture, the better you cover the paper, the more realistic your drawing.

TIP - Keep your pencils sharp. It will help you cover the paper better.

TIP - Draw light and layer your colors. Remember that color pencil is semi-transparent.

TIP - White is an excellent blending color. Remember you mix your colors on the paper.

TIP - Use clear acetate under your hand. It does not smear the colors and you can see through it.

TIP - An ebony pencil is an excellent tool to add details.

TIP - A white gel pen works great to add highlights.

TIP - Do not worry about mistakes, work around them.

TIP - Indigo Blue is an excellent color to darken green.

TIP - A colorless blender pen works great to blend colors.

TIP - When starting a drawing, start on what you think is the hardest part. Only move on when you are satisfied with that portion.

TIP - Use the grid method, it makes what you have to do more manageable.

TIP - When drawing on black paper, remember you cannot erase, it will scuff the paper.

TIP - When drawing from a photograph, remember it is only for reference. Do not let it determine your final result.

TIP - Drawing with color pencil requires patience, IT WILL TAKE TIME.

TIP - Using markers is an excellent way to under-paint parts of your drawing.

TIP - Art Stixs are an excellent way add a different texture to your drawing.

TIP - When finished with your final art, spray it with a final gloss or matt finish. It will enhance the colors and help preserve your work.